Translation and Multilingual Natural Language Processing

In this series:

1. Fantinuoli, Claudio & Federico Zanettin (eds.). New directions in corpus-based translation studies.
2. Hansen-Schirra, Silvia & Sambor Grucza (eds.). Eyetracking and Applied Linguistics.
3. Neumann, Stella, Oliver Čulo & Silvia Hansen-Schirra (eds.). Annotation, exploitation and evaluation of parallel corpora: TC3 I.
4. Czulo, Oliver & Silvia Hansen-Schirra (eds.). Crossroads between Contrastive Linguistics, Translation Studies and Machine Translation: TC3 II.
5. Rehm, Georg, Felix Sasaki, Daniel Stein & Andreas Witt (eds.). Language technologies for a multilingual Europe: TC3 III.
6. Menzel, Katrin, Ekaterina Lapshinova-Koltunski & Kerstin Anna Kunz (eds.). New perspectives on cohesion and coherence: Implications for translation.
7. Hansen-Schirra, Silvia, Oliver Czulo, Sascha Hofmann & Bernd Meyer (eds). Empirical modelling of translation and interpreting.
8. Svoboda, Tomáš, Łucja Biel & Krzysztof Łoboda (eds.). Quality aspects in institutional translation.

ISSN: 2364-8899

Quality aspects in institutional translation

Edited by

Tomáš Svoboda

Lucja Biel

Krzysztof Łoboda

Tomáš Svoboda, Łucja Biel & Krzysztof Łoboda (eds.). 2017. *Quality aspects in institutional translation* (Translation and Multilingual Natural Language Processing 8). Berlin: Language Science Press.

This title can be downloaded at: http://langsci-press.org/catalog/book/181

Published in cooperation with the European Commission (for further details, please consult page v).
Published in collaboration with JTP - Jednota tlumočníků a překladatelů (Czech Association of Translators and Interpreters), Prague 2017.

ISBN: 978-3-946234-83-8 (Digital)
978-3-96110-021-7 (Hardcover)
978-80-7374-125-9 (JTP) (Softcover)
ISSN: 2364-8899
DOI:10.5281/zenodo.1048173
Source code available from www.github.com/langsci/181
Collaborative reading: paperhive.org/documents/remote?type=langsci&id=181
Cover and concept of design: Ulrike Harbort
Typesetting: Sebastian Nordhoff, Iana Stefanova
Proofreading: Amr Zawawy, Caroline Rossi, Jeroen van de Weijer, Prisca Jerono, Sebastian Nordhoff
Fonts: Linux Libertine, Arimo, DejaVu Sans Mono
Typesetting software: XƎLaTeX

Language Science Press
Unter den Linden 6
10099 Berlin, Germany
langsci-press.org

Storage and cataloguing done by FU Berlin

Contents

This book was published with the financial support of the European Commission under the Translating Europe project.

The information and views set out in this publication are those of the authors and do not necessarily reflect the official opinion of the European Union. Neither the European Union institutions and bodies nor any person acting on their behalf may be held responsible for the use which may be made of the information contained therein.

Notes on editors and contributors

John L. Beaven

After obtaining a PhD in Machine Translation from Edinburgh University, John Beaven worked as a computational linguistics researcher in academia (University of Cambridge) and industry (Sharp Laboratories of Europe, Oxford) in the fields of MT and linguistic databases. Since 1996, he has been working in the translation departments of different European Union institutions and bodies, at first in the fields of MT and the deployment of CAT tools. He is currently responsible for the Quality Policy at the Translation Service of the General Secretariat of the Council of the European Union (EU).

Łucja Biel

Łucja Biel is an Associate Professor at the Institute of Applied Linguistics, University of Warsaw, Poland, where she teaches and researches legal translation. She is Secretary General of the European Society of Translation Studies (EST) and a deputy editor of the Journal of Specialised Translation. She was a Visiting Lecturer on the MA in Legal Translation at City University London from 2009 to 2014. She holds an MA in Translation Studies (Jagiellonian University of Kraków), PhD in Linguistics (University of Gdańsk), and Diploma in English and EU Law (University of Cambridge) and a School of American Law diploma (Chicago-Kent School of Law and University of Gdańsk). She has participated in a number of internationally and nationally funded research projects and has published widely in the area of EU/legal translation, translator training and corpus linguistics, including a book *Lost in the Eurofog. The Textual Fit of Translated Law* (Peter Lang, 2014).

Jan Hanzl

Jan Hanzl graduated from the Faculty of International Relations at the University of Economics in Prague and from the Faculty of Arts at the Charles University in Prague. Between 2004 and 2007 he worked as a reviser at the Office of the Government of the Czech Republic in a department responsible for the translation of EU legislation adopted before the accession of the Czech Republic to the EU, and as a freelance translator for EU institutions. Since 2007 he has been working as a translator at the General Secretariat of the Council of the EU.

Dariusz Koźbiał

Dariusz Koźbiał is a PhD candidate at the Faculty of Applied Linguistics, University of Warsaw, Poland, writing a thesis entitled Translation of Judgments: A Corpus Study of the Textual Fit of EU to Polish Judgments. In 2015, he graduated from the Institute of Applied Linguistics, University of Warsaw, with an MA in Applied Linguistics (English, German). He completed a three-month translation traineeship in the Directorate-General for Translation at the European Parliament in Luxembourg. He is involved as an investigator in a research project "The Eurolect: An EU variant of Polish and its impact on administrative Polish" funded by the Polish National Science Centre. His research interests include legal translation, institutional translation and corpus linguistics.

Krzysztof Łoboda

Krzysztof Łoboda is a translator trainer and researcher at the Jagiellonian University in Kraków, where he earned an MA in Translation Studies to further continue PhD studies in linguistics. He has also completed postgraduate studies in Research Project Management and other courses such as Term Extraction and Management at Imperial College London. He is a member of the PKN Technical Committee 256 on Terminology, Other Language Resources and Content Management. Since 2004 Krzysztof has been an external translator/reviser of documents issued by EU institutions (mostly EC, but also EP, CoR and EESC). His research interests include translation technology, specialized translation, and e-learning in translator training. He is currently involved in developing TRALICE consortium of translation professionals and researchers, a regional platform to facilitate cooperation between business and academia.

Fernando Prieto Ramos

Fernando Prieto Ramos is Full Professor of Translation and Director of the Centre for Legal and Institutional Translation Studies (Transius) at the University of Geneva's Faculty of Translation and Interpreting. With a background in both Translation and Law, his work focuses on legal and institutional translation, including interdisciplinary methodologies, international legal instruments and specialized terminology. Former member of the Centre for Translation and Textual Studies at Dublin City University, he has published widely on legal translation, and has received several research and teaching awards, including a European Label Award for Innovative Methods in Language Teaching from the European Commission, an International Geneva Award from the Swiss Network for International Studies and a Consolidator Grant for his project on "Legal Translation in International Institutional Settings" (LETRINT). He has also translated for several organizations since 1997, including five years as an in-house translator at the World Trade Organization (dispute settlement team).

Karolina Stefaniak

Karolina Stefaniak is a linguist and translator. She obtained her PhD from University of Warsaw in 2008 with a dissertation in the field of critical discourse analysis on the communication between doctors and patients. Since 2008 she has been working in the Polish Language Department of the Directorate-General for Translation (DGT) of the European Commission in Luxembourg, first as a translator, then as the main terminologist and currently as a quality officer. She has published several articles on doctor-patient interaction, medical discourse and medicalization, and also on specialized and institutional translation, including translation in EU institutions.

Ingemar Strandvik

Ingemar Strandvik works as a quality manager at the European Commission's Directorate-General for Translation, where he was formerly a translator. He has a background as a state-authorized legal translator and court interpreter in Sweden, where he also taught translation at Stockholm University and participated in curriculum design for Translation Studies. For many years he was active as a lexicographer at the publishing house Norstedts. Apart from studies in Philology and degrees in Translation and Interpreting, he has a Master's degree in EU Law. He is currently involved in standardization work and regularly participates in conferences and publishes on translation quality, multilingual law-making and terminology.

Tomáš Svoboda

Tomáš Svoboda is Head of German Department in the Institute of Translation Studies, Charles University, Prague, Czech Republic, from which he graduated in English and German translation. He earned his Ph.D. in Translation Studies in 2004. From 2004 to 2007 Tomáš worked as an in-house translator and training coordinator for the Czech Language Department of the Directorate-General for Translation, European Commission, Luxembourg, and subsequently for four years as a contractor for the European Central Bank in Frankfurt, Germany. He lectures on technical and institutional translation, translation tools and technologies, and translation history in the Institute of Translation Studies. He is an active translator and auditor under the ISO 17100 standard. His publications cover translation quality, institutional and technical translation, translation technology, future of the translation profession as well as translation history. Tomáš is member of the Executive Board of the Czech Union of Translators and Interpreters, a coordinator of FIT Europe (Fédération Internationale des Traducteurs) Technology Group, and Board Member of the European Masters in Translation (EMT) network.

Sonia Vandepitte

Sonia Vandepitte is a Full Professor at the Department of Translation, Interpreting and Communication at Ghent University and head of its English section. She teaches English, Translation Studies, and translation into and from Dutch. Publication topics include causal expressions in language and translation, methodology in Translation Studies, translation competences, anticipation in interpreting, international translation teaching projects and translation and post-editing processes. She is currently involved in eye-tracking research into reading and translation processes of translation problem-solving. She is also investigating peer feedback and other collaborative forms of learning in translation training and co-editing the Handbook of Research on Multilingual Writing and Pedagogical Cooperation in Virtual Learning Environments and Quality Assurance and Assessment Practices in Translation and Interpreting.

Acknowledgements

This book is published under the open-access scheme in online form. In addition, thanks to the funding obtained from the European Commission to cover production costs, the book will be printed in 250 copies at the end of 2017. The print version of the book will be distributed free of charge throughout Europe to relevant libraries and universities. The European Commission's funding also covered the Kraków and Prague conferences held as part of the Translating Europe project.

We wish to thank the publishing house Language Science Press, whose publishing project is concerned not only with Linguistics, but also, among other fields of enquiry, with Translation Studies. Language Science Press's lean structure made it possible to flexibly cater for our needs to publish the book within considerable time and cost constraints.

The editors wish to thank all the numerous peer reviewers who reviewed and commented on individual contributions.

Chapter 1

Quality aspects in institutional translation: Introduction

Tomáš Svoboda
Charles University, Prague

Łucja Biel
University of Warsaw

Krzysztof Łoboda
Jagiellonian University, Kraków

1 Introduction

Quality has been on translation scholars' minds since the emergence of Translation Studies (TS) as a discipline in the 1970s, with one of the seminal monographs by Juliane House being published in 1977. More recently, with TS shifting its focus to integrate non-literary texts more broadly (cf. Rogers 2015), the quality aspect has been researched across various specialized fields and genres. One of these fields is Institutional Translation, where the quest for product and process quality underlies the *raison d'être* of in-house translation teams. This field requires further in-depth research into quality aspects to combine and cross-fertilize theory and practice.

The purpose of this collective monograph is to explore key issues, approaches and challenges to quality in institutional translation by confronting academics' and practitioners' perspectives. What the reader will find in this book is an interplay of two approaches: academic contributions providing the conceptual and theoretical background for discussing quality on the one hand, and chapters exploring selected aspects of quality and case studies from both academics and

Tomáš Svoboda, Łucja Biel & Krzysztof Łoboda. 2017. Quality aspects in institutional translation: Introduction. In Tomáš Svoboda, Łucja Biel & Krzysztof Łoboda (eds.), *Quality aspects in institutional translation*, 1–13. Berlin: Language Science Press. DOI:10.5281/zenodo.1048175

practitioners, on the other hand. Our aim is to present these two approaches as a breeding ground for testing one vis-à-vis the other.

This book studies institutional translation mostly[1] through the lens of the European Union (EU) reality, and, more specifically, of EU institutions and bodies, due to the unprecedented scale of their multilingual operations and the legal and political importance of translation. Thus, it is concerned with the supranational (international) level, deliberately leaving national[2] and other contexts aside. Quality in supranational institutions is explored both in terms of translation processes and products – the translated texts.

2 Kraków and Prague TEW conferences as an initial stage for the book project

This collective monograph is inspired, partially, by two conferences held as part of a joint Translating Europe Workshop event[3] supported by the European Commission's Directorate-General for Translation (DGT): a conference entitled *Points of View on Translator's Competence and Translation Quality* held in Kraków in November 2015 and the *Quality Aspects in Institutional Translation* conference held in Prague in November 2016. The former was organised with the aim of attracting a broad audience of both Translation Studies scholars and translation practitioners to tackle the concept of quality from as many angles as possible while the Prague follow-up built up on its findings and focused narrowly on quality in supranational institutions. Selected speakers were invited to contribute to this collective monograph with its overarching theme of quality. Subsequently, the invitation was extended to a few academics and practitioners working in this area.

[1]Except for Prieto Ramos' and Vandepitte's chapters which also survey supranational, intergovernmental and/or centralised national organizations.

[2]See Svoboda (2017) for literature review of quality aspects in national institutional translation settings.

[3]The event was held under the #TranslatingEurope project, which aims to bring together stakeholders in the translation profession across Europe. The project consists of the yearly forum organised in Brussels and the workshops, which are smaller events (conferences, seminars, round tables) targeted towards more regional level, at specialised audiences. The workshops are often organised in cooperation with EMT (European Master's in Translation) universities.

3 Institutional translation and quality: basic concepts

This book addresses the institutional nature of translations, which has been acknowledged to be "a neglected factor" in Translation Studies (cf. Mason 2004 [2003]: 470). *Institutional translation* can be defined in broad or narrow terms. We adopt Schäffner et al.'s definition, which seems to represent a balanced account:

> In the widest sense, any translation that occurs in an institutional setting can be called institutional translation, and consequently the institution that manages translation is a translating institution. In Translation Studies, however, the label "institutional translation" is generally used to refer to translating in or for a specific organisation… Institutional translation is typically collective, anonymous and standardised. (2014: 493–494)

As Schäffner et al. argue, the fact that institutional translation is "typically collective, anonymous and standardised" (2014: 494) requires institutions to ensure the lexical, grammatical and stylistic consistency of translations. Such standardization is achieved through "style guides and CAT tools, revision procedures, and mentoring and training arrangements" (ibid.). Thus, standardization may be regarded as one of the defining features of institutional translation.

Given the divergent conceptualizations of the term 'institutional translation' and the narrow grounds against which the term was initially coined (i.e. supranational institutions, especially institutions/bodies of the EU), Koskinen (2014) addresses the definition of institutional translation through the question of "what purpose(s) translation serves in institutions" (2014: 480) and studies the topic of governance in the context of translating institutions. Her approach is inspirational in two ways: it offers a way of approximating divergent research endeavours in the field and, beyond that, it offers a broad platform to interpret research results.

The present book is an in-depth consideration of one of the many aspects of institutional translation – yet one of key importance – both as regards research and translation practice within institutions – namely quality. *Quality* can be defined in many ways. In the industrial/commercial practice, with which institutional contexts tend to have increasingly more in common (cf. Mossop 2006), quality – in connection with the ISO 9000 standards (cf. ISO 9000:2015 2015) – is often understood as a degree to which the inherent characteristics of a product or a process fulfil the clients' expectations.

An important distinction which is made in the literature and in the translation industry (cf. Drugan 2013) holds between *quality assessment*, that is attempts at objective measurements of quality of translated texts, versus *quality assurance*, that is systematic attempts at controlling the quality of processes[4]. This book is concerned both with the quality of the translation process, including quality management policies, and – on a conceptual plane – with the outcome of the translation process, i.e. translation products (cf. mainly Vandepitte, in this volume). The process-oriented approach is linked with the notion of quality assurance (QA), which Mossop (2001) defines as:

> ... the full set of procedures applied before, during and after the translation production process, by all members of a translating organisation, to ensure that quality objectives important to clients are being met. Quality assurance includes procedures to ensure [...] [q]uality of service [...,] [q]uality of the physical product [... and] [q]uality of the translation. [...] Where work is being done on contract, quality assurance includes selecting the best contractor. (2001: 92–93)

Thus, quality assurance is understood in a holistic way to cover all stages of translation provision. This collective monograph adopts Mossop's broad definition to explore how – in order to assure and control the quality of translations as products – institutions control processes, people and resources, including the hiring of quality managers (Prieto Ramos, this volume), terminology management (Stefaniak, this volume), standardization through style guides and translation manuals (Svoboda, this volume), as well as outsourcing evaluation (Strandvik, this volume), to name but a few of the aspects at hand.

4 Research on institutional translation through the lens of quality

Quality aspects of translation at international/supranational level have been researched theoretically (cf. Prieto Ramos 2015) and practically, mainly in the context of the United Nations (UN) and the European Union (EU).

In respect of the UN, De Saint Robert (2009) details UN's approach to translation quality assessment, pointing out client orientedness as a major component of the UN communication strategy. Didaoui (2009) locates the role of UN

[4]See Drugan for an overview and differences between the academia and the industry (2013: 35–38), as well as for definitions of related terms: quality assurance, quality evaluation, quality control, quality assurance, quality planning and quality improvement (2013: 76–77).

translators in the UN translation quality management (QM) system, thus putting the person of a translator in the foreground. The focus on human resources is maintained in a PhD dissertation by Lafeber (2012), who focuses on skills and knowledge required of translators and revisers in 24 inter-governmental organizations and correlates her findings with recruitment tests at such organizations, particularly with some insider knowledge from the UN translation service.

As for the EU, the topic of quality has been given more attention in recent years with a growing number of publications, both by academics and EU institutions. In respect of products, Koskinen (2008: 104–106) approaches translation quality from the point of view of readability. A similar focus may be observed in empirical studies which analyze the textual fit of translations against national conventions for specific genres, e.g. multilingual legislation (Biel 2014). Another textual-level aspect concerns terminological consistency of EU translations (Pacho 2017). Quite a few studies approach quality from the process perspective. A practical example of a guideline in translation quality in an institutional setting provides the European Commission DGT (2009). Another practice-oriented resource is the European Commission's study (DGT 2012), which quantifies, among other things, potential losses in scenarios when less ambitious quality assurance measures would be applied within the Directorate-General for Translation (DGT). Similarly to Didaoui (2009) and the way he discribes the UN translation department, Svoboda (2008) follows the same aim of locating the individual within the quality management system within the DGT workflow. A review of the translation quality requirements with EU institutions' outsourcing procedures is given in Sosoni (2011). Most recently, Strandvik (2015; 2017) and Drugan et al. (2018) demonstrate the evolution of the approach to quality assurance in the European Commission, evidence the changing significance and definition of quality into fitness for purpose. Fitness for purpose emphasizes the scalability of quality (a concept which has its roots in the Skopos theory and its idea of degrees of translation adequacy, cf. Nord 2010: 122) and allows institutions to prioritize certain aspects of quality, balancing political and legal risks with available resources.

Yet, despite the growing number of publications on the topic of quality, there is still a dearth of empirical and narrowly-focused studies, discussing aspects of quality in a systematic way. This publication aspires to be a step forward towards filling in the niche.

5 Structure of the book

This book, which brings together eight contributions revolving around the central topic of (process/product) quality in institutional translation, is organized into three parts. The first part (Vandepitte, Biel) sets the conceptual and theoretical background for the study, identifying main components of quality in the institutional context. The next part studies selected aspects of quality assurance – quality managers (Prieto Ramos), style guides (Svoboda), terminology management (Stefaniak) and outsourcing evaluation (Strandvik). The last part contains empirical studies on two institutions – the Council and the Court of Justice (Hanzl and Beaven, Koźbiał). Contributions by practitioners (Stefaniak, Strandvik, Hanzl and Beaven) serve as a "reality check" for academic contributions, by describing quality procedures in major EU institutions (The European Commission, the Council and the Court).

The authors and editors come from 7 institutions, of which there are five universities (Charles University, Prague, Ghent University, University of Geneva, Warsaw University, Jagiellonian University) and two EU institutions, i.e. the Translation Service of the General Secretariat of the Council of the EU and the European Commission's Directorate-General for Translation.

6 Overview of individual chapters

The conceptual part opens with a chapter authored by Sonia **Vandepitte** from Ghent University (chapter title: "Translation product quality: A conceptual analysis"), who sets the ground for the ensuing discussions by reviewing the fundamental concepts related to quality. The chapter is adjusted to the actual (and broad) background of institutional translation, in which both the translation product and translation process have a role to play. Against this backdrop, Vandepitte deals extensively with the topic of translation quality assessment (TQA) with respect to the translation product. To this end, she employs the following parameters: the object, the purpose, and the criteria/quality levels of translation quality assessment (including their scaling and weighting), as well as the actors involved. She also raises the question (albeit as a one-off consideration) of cognitive processes implied in TQA – an aspect which most of TQA-related studies have neglected to consider so far. The chapter reflects in more detail on the actors involved in TQA, a vital feature to be tackled in the introductory chapter. She illustrates the use of parameters on the workings of a national institution (SCTA, the central translation service for German in Belgium). The chapter is both conceptual and empirical (SCTA survey) and, in its concluding part, is applicable in practice, too, thanks to a model where Vandepitte presents the above parameters as part of a coherent system. This makes the opening chapter a valuable asset in the bi-directional process of exchange between (Translation Studies) theory and (translation) practice.

In the second conceptual chapter, Łucja **Biel** from the University of Warsaw (chapter title: "Quality in institutional EU Translation: Parameters, policies and practices") identifies key quality parameters of EU translation. Biel does so by analyzing and evaluating institutional policies as well as practices. Besides that, she compares and contrasts this view with the pertinent academic literature. The chapter deals with quality on two interrelated and overlapping planes: that of the textual level (where translations are viewed as products and are judged with the criteria of equivalence, consistency/continuity, on the one hand, and of textual fit and clarity on the other hand) and that of the process level (where translation is viewed as a service), which subsumes workflow management, human resources and tools. She observes that, recently, EU institutions have foregrounded quality aspects. This is particularly visible at the European Commission's DGT, where the quality discourse has been reframed by linking translation quality (at the textual level) to genres and genre clusters, which has raised the visibility of the criterion of clarity. This shift is, most likely, effected by a managerial approach to assuring translation (product) quality and the concept of fit-for-purpose translations as part of what DGT refers to as Total Quality Management (TQM).

The next part of the book opens with the contribution by Fernando **Prieto Ramos** from the University of Geneva, entitled "The evolving role of institutional translation service managers in quality assurance: Profiles and challenges". Adopting a holistic approach to translation quality, this chapter foregrounds a neglected and under-researched component of quality assurance – namely, profiles of senior and mid-level translation service managers, that is translation service directors and heads of language units, who take fundamental decisions that affect the day-to-day management of translation units. Prieto Ramos surveys and contrasts the management structures at twelve intergovernmental and supranational organizations and studies their job descriptions in vacancy notices. The common ground in the scope of duties across the organizations is discussed around four groups: (1) strategic, administrative and financial matters; (2) staffing matters; (3) translation workflow coordination, and (4) contribution to translation, technical and quality control tasks. His study shows a reorientation from "one-fits-all quality control to a more modulated approach to quality variables". The second part of the paper reports on structured interviews with service managers with a focus on quality assurance practices and challenges. The key interrelated challenges to quality are related to: (1) resource availability and productivity pressures due to cost-effective measures and budget limitations; (2) outsourcing procedures; and (3) workflow changes caused by technological developments, including new error patterns and new variables in the workflow. Prieto Ramos concludes with recommendations for an adequate balance between service managers' translation expertise and managerial skills.

The next chapter by Tomáš **Svoboda** from Charles University, Prague, entitled "Translation manuals and style guides as quality assurance indicators: The case of the European Commission's Directorate-General for Translation" asks to what extent the quality aspect of institutional translation is governed by rules, analyzing it through the prism of translation manuals and style guides. In his empirical quantitative study, Svoboda surveys 24 language pages of the DGT's resource website, which is the largest resource of its kind, and contrasts the number and type of resources across language units, demonstrating shared areas and variation of language-specific resources up to 50% of the links analyzed. The findings indicate that the structure and content of resources is largely standardized and harmonized, in particular as regards EU information – namely references to EU institutions, terminology resources and the Interinstitutional Style Guide. The highest variation was identified for language-specific resources, with significant differences between individual languages. The analysis of the content of link tags shows that resources are assigned a large variety of 'labels', ranging from names which strongly suggest the binding status of resources (e.g. decree, rules, instructions, requirements) to names which connote their less pressing nature (e.g. recommendations, tips, advice). In conclusions Svoboda comments on the complexity of institutional translation: "for their translations to be considered high quality, the translators (...) have to follow very many recommendations and instructions".

Another related aspect of quality assurance – terminology management – is undertaken in the contribution by Karolina **Stefaniak**, a terminologist at the European Commission's DGT ("Terminology work in the European Commission: Ensuring high-quality translation in a multilingual environment"). Stefaniak documents the daily work of a terminologist – a separate role assisting translators in terminological searches – on the example of the DGT's Polish Language Department. The chapter explores the specificity of EU terminology, in particular, its supranational peculiarity, highly specialized or novel nature, occasional intended ambiguity, political sensitiveness and, last but not least, its systemic nature which requires terms to be internally consistent. Interestingly, Stefaniak reports that the majority (90%) of translators' queries deal with scientific terms rather than with legal terms which tend to be rare. The second part of the paper discusses criteria and techniques applied when solving terminological problems in the EU context. The author observes a strong preference for literal translation techniques, descriptive equivalents and neologisms. As for the quality criteria in the terminological decision-making process, they include accuracy, clarity and internal consistency of terminology, which often overrides other considerations. The standardization of terminology in translations is also achieved through terminological resources, including the IATE termbase, a major terminological achievement of EU institutions.

The next chapter by Ingemar **Strandvik**, a quality officer from the European Commission's DGT ("Evaluation of outsourced translations. State of play in the European Commission's Directorate-General for Translation (DGT)") addresses a novel and underresearched topic of evaluating outsourced translations, a trend gaining recently in importance in EU institutions due to budgetary constraints and limited human resources. Strandvik shares his insider knowledge of evaluation practices in the DGT, including assessment tools and the evaluation grid. The chapter draws attention to many outsourcing challenges, such as (1) the need to ensure the consistency of evaluation practice among 1600 in-house translators; (2) differences in the size of translation markets in various Member States; (3) time allocated for revision and evaluation; and (4) risks involved in mistranslation. These and other factors have contributed to the evolution of the reference model for translation quality management, and to a move from the fidelity to fitness-for-purpose approach to quality. Strandvik raises an important point of missing empirical evidence as to the correlation between sample sizes and assessment reliability. The chapter ends with a pertinent discussion on recent developments and further challenges related to translation evaluation and ensuring a translation quality policy at the interinstitutional level.

In their case study entitled "Quality assurance at the Council of the EU's Translation Service", Jan **Hanzl** and John **Beaven** from the Council's General Secretariat offer an insider view on quality practices and policies within the Council, an institution which is far less outspoken about its quality policies compared to the European Commission. The authors discuss the specificity of translation work at the Council related in particular to the fact that texts are subject to numerous discussions and amendments until their content is supported by the Member States. Thus, translators rarely translate from scratch but work on interim and working texts at various stages of their amendment ("versions drawn up in a hurry by non-native English speakers, not final, well-edited and fine-tuned texts"), often against tight deadlines. Similarly to Stefaniak, the authors emphasize the importance of continuity and consistency at the terminological and phraseological level, both within a document and across related documents. Working in such a specific environment, the Council has adopted a pragmatic approach to quality based on the fit for purpose principle correlated with revision levels adjusted to the political visibility and legal/financial impact of text types in order to ensure "an optimal level of useful quality". Quality requirements are divided into three sets of criteria: (1) linguistic aspects, including accuracy, clarity and fluency; (2) technical aspects, including the parallel pagination of language versions for practical reasons; and (3) timeliness to ensure the smooth operation of the Council. The authors conclude with the description of the Council's ex-post quality monitoring system designed in 2009 to regularly and systematically evaluate translation samples.

Last but not least, the final case study addresses quality at the Court of Justice of the European Union (CJEU). Dariusz **Koźbiał** from the University of Warsaw focuses on key aspects underlying the Quality Assurance strategy in this multilingual and supranational judiciary institution. In the introductory section of the chapter "A two-tiered approach to quality assurance in legal translation at the Court of Justice of the European Union", Koźbiał discusses the complexity of current language arrangements in the CJEU and the specificity of translations (their predominant legal nature) in this institution, drawing attention to the fact that "the goal of translation at the CJEU is to produce parallel texts that will allow uniform interpretation and application by national courts". The main part of the chapter proposes a two-tiered approach to translation quality at the CJEU, which can be conceptualized at two interrelated levels, i.e. human resources and workflow. The former level comprises in-house lawyer-linguists, external contractors, revisers, auxiliary staff and project managers, whereas the latter consists of measures related to the translation process as well as intra- and interinstitutional co-operation.

7 Conclusions

This volume aims at contributing to the deeper understanding of institutional translation, mainly, but not exclusively in the domain of EU translation. By presenting a blend of conceptual and empirical studies, this collective monograph intends to offer an extension to research available so far, which is still far from being saturated. As Schäffner et al. put it, "[t]here is widespread agreement among researchers [...] that institutional translation is still rather unexplored and that empirical studies are missing" (2014: 494); similar remarks may also be observed in some chapters by the practitioners who contributed to this book. Likewise, the proposed reconciliation of both the academic and the professional views is suggested as a continuation of a dialogue, which has the potential of enriching and cross-fertilizing both areas. The discipline of Translation Studies is a witness to a bi-directional movement of academic reflection informing practical decisions of professionals on the one hand, and, on the other, observations from practice providing solid grounds and data for academic research.

References

Biel, Łucja. 2014. *Lost in the Eurofog: the textual fit of translated law.* Frankfurt am Main: Peter Lang.

De Saint Robert, Maria-Josée. 2009. Assessing quality in translation and terminology at the United Nations. In Martin Forstner, Hanna Lee-Jahnke & Peter A. Schmitt (eds.), *Ciuti-forum 2008: enhancing translation quality: ways, means, methods,* 387–392. New York: Peter Lang.

Didaoui, Mohammed. 2009. Managing quality and inequality in institutional translation services. In Martin Forstner, Hanna Lee-Jahnke & Peter A. Schmitt (eds.), *CIUTI-Forum 2008: Enhancing translation quality: Ways, means, methods,* 345–364. New York: Peter Lang.

Directorate-General for Translation (DGT), European Commission. 2009. *Programme for Quality Management in Translation – 22 Quality Actions.* http://translationjournal.net/e-Books/programme-for-quality-management-in-translation.html, accessed 2017-9-30.

Drugan, Joanna. 2013. *Quality in professional translation: assessment and improvement.* London: Bloomsbury.

Drugan, Joanna, Ingemar Strandvik & Erkka Vuorinen. 2018. Translation quality, quality management and agency: principles and practice in the European Union institutions. In Joss Moorkens, Sheila Castilho, Stephen Doherty & Federico Gaspari (eds.), *Translation quality assessment: from principles to practice.* Berlin: Springer.

ISO 9000:2015. 2015. *Quality management systems – Fundamentals and vocabulary.* Geneva: ISO.

Koskinen, Kaisa. 2008. *Translating institutions. an ethnographic study of EU translation.* Manchester: St. Jerome.

Koskinen, Kaisa. 2014. Institutional translation: the art of government by translation. *Perspectives: Studies in Translatology* 22(4). 479–492.

Lafeber, Anne. 2012. *Translation at inter-governmental organizations: the set of skills and knowledge required and the implications for recruitment testing*. Universitat Rovira i Virgili doctoral dissertation.

Mason, Ian. 2004 [2003]. Text parameters in translation: transitivity and institutional cultures. In Lawrence Venuti (ed.), *The translation studies reader*, 2nd edn., 470–481. New York/London: Routledge.

Mossop, Brian. 2001. *Revising and editing for translators*. 1st edn. Manchester: St. Jerome Publishing.

Mossop, Brian. 2006. From culture to business. *The Translator* 12(1). 1–27. DOI:10.1080/13556509.2006.10799207

Nord, Christiane. 2010. Functionalist approaches. In Yves Gambier & Luc van Doorslaer (eds.), *Handbook of translation studies*, vol. 1, 120–128. Amsterdam: John Benjamins.

Pacho, Lucie. 2017. Promoting multilingual consistency for the quality of EU law. *International Journal for the Semiotics of Law* 30. 67–79.

Prieto Ramos, Fernando. 2015. Quality assurance in legal translation: evaluating process, competence and product in the pursuit of adequacy. *International Journal for the Semiotics of Law* 28. 11–30.

Rogers, Margaret. 2015. *Specialised translation: shedding the 'non-literary' tag*. London: Routledge.

Schäffner, Christina, Luciana Sabina Tcaciuc & Wine Tesseur. 2014. Translation practices in political institutions: a comparison of national, supranational, and non-governmental organisations. *Perspectives. Studies in Translatology* 22(4). 493–510. DOI:10.1080/0907676X.2014.948890

Sosoni, Vilelmini. 2011. Training translators to work for the EU institutions: luxury or necessity. *The Journal of Specialised Translation* 16. 77–108.

Strandvik, Ingemar. 2015. On quality in EU multilingual lawmaking. In Susan Šarčević (ed.), *Language and culture in EU Law. Multidisciplinary perspectives*, 141–165. Farnham: Ashgate.

Strandvik, Ingemar. 2017. Towards a more structured approach to quality assurance: DGT's quality journey. In Fernando Prieto Ramos (ed.), *Institutional translation for international governance: enhancing quality in multilingual legal communication*, 51–62. London: Bloomsbury.

Svoboda, Tomáš. 2008. Ubi sunt homines? Poznámky k řízení kvality překladů u Generálního ředitelství pro překlad Evropské komise [Ubi sunt homines? On Translation Quality Management at the European Commission's Directorate-General for Translation]. In Alena Ďuricová (ed.), *Od textu k prekladu II*, 143–151. Prague: Jednota tlumočníků a překladatelů.

Svoboda, Tomáš. 2017. Translation manuals and style guides as quality assurance indicators: The case of the European Commission's Directorate-General for Translation. In Tomáš Svoboda, Łucja Biel & Krzysztof Łoboda (eds.), *Quality aspects in institutional translation* (Translation and Multilingual Natural Language Processing 8), 75–107. Berlin: Language Science Press. DOI:10.5281/zenodo.1048190

Chapter 2

Translation product quality: A conceptual analysis

Sonia Vandepitte
Ghent University

Against a background in which both the translation product and translation process are briefly described as objects of quality assessment, this chapter presents an analysis of the concept of translation quality assessment focussing on the translation product. The following features will be presented as parameters along which product quality assessment practices in institutions can be described: the purpose of translation quality assessment, the criteria applied in the assessment, combined with their scaling and weighting, the translation quality levels aimed at, and the quality assessors involved. The characteristics will be illustrated by the translation quality assessment as applied in one Belgian institution. It is hoped that the analysis will lead to a fuller and deeper understanding of a translation's quality.

1 The object of translation quality assessment: translation product and translation process

In June 2015, a translation error delayed the renovation of Brussels opera hall De Munt / La Monnaie: planned renovations were postponed by four months. They should have started in June 2015, but could not because of an error in the translation that had legal consequences. In the public procurement, the Dutch phrase *scenische werken* ('scene works') was translated as *des travaux scénographiques* ('scenographic works'). In French, that description apparently also potentially has an artistic meaning and can be interpreted as meaning that the opera hall could employ a renovation company for artistic purposes. One consequence was that De Munt productions were to be seen at other locations in the city, but another consequence was also that a fair number of season ticket holders preferred

Sonia Vandepitte. 2017. Translation product quality: A conceptual analysis. In Tomáš Svoboda, Łucja Biel & Krzysztof Łoboda (eds.), *Quality aspects in institutional translation*, 15–29. Berlin: Language Science Press. DOI:10.5281/zenodo.1048180

to skip a season. Avoiding such – and any other – textual translation errors is most important to organizations, especially when it comes to sensitive documents or high risk communication and will be the main topic of this chapter.

However, before I narrow down the scope to the translation product, another potential object of a quality assessment in the translation environment needs to be mentioned, i.e. the translation process. Let us first look at the following case, exemplified by a traffic sign in Swansea that revealed problems of a non-textual nature as reported by the BBC (BBC-News 2008). While English-speaking motorists may well have understood the sign saying *No entry for heavy goods vehicles. Residential site only*, monolingual Welsh lorry drivers must have been at a loss when they read *Nid wyf yn y swyddfa ar hyn o bryd. Anfonwch unrhyw waith i'w gyfieithu*, which translates as 'I am not in the office at the moment. Please send any work to be translated.' Here, the translation error did not result from a translator making an error during the micro-process of translating, but it resulted from poor translation management skills and a poor translation quality assurance process. The error was mentioned on BBC-News, Radio 4, on 31 October 2008: the sign was posted by Swansea Council, obviously commissioned by someone who did not know Welsh and therefore did not apply the required translation management skills. In other words, the macro-process of providing for the appropriate people to deal with the production of the translation failed, resulting in an inappropriate end product.

The difference between the two potential objects of a translation quality assessment, the translation product and the translation process, may also be illustrated by means of the following question: does the quality assessment concern the translation product only or does it also include aspects from the translation cognitive or textual process or the translation service? In other words, is it the translated text only that is assessed or does the assessment also include the way in which the translator(s) produced the text, or the "core processes, resources, and other aspects necessary for the delivery of a quality translation service that meets applicable specifications" (ISO 17100:2015 2015) or even the manner in which the translation is brought to the recipient?

Such differences in quality assessment need to be identified clearly in the assessment as the first step in a translation quality assessment exercise: Is an institution interested in improving its procedures for producing higher quality translations or does it want to raise the quality of the final translations? Does an institution wish to identify the best translation produced by different people or does it wish to determine which are the best company processes that will guarantee high-quality translations?

The borderline between product and process issues is, however, not straightforward. Some characteristics, such as "punctuality", "proactivity", or "initiative in upgrading the terminology", can, indeed, only be related to one object, in case the processes that are part of the service provision. Other matters, however, like, for instance, "compliance with a style guide",[1] could both apply to a translator's acts, and be considered a process issue, and to the translation itself, and be regarded as a product issue. In addition, textual errors – whichever way they have been produced – can always be related to some process irregularity whether at the micro-level or at the macro-level and the translation product quality will invariably be relatable to the quality of the process. Hence, a study of the former may also reveal information about the latter, and the concept of *translation quality* may often include references to issues of both products and processes, leaving it up to the reader or listener to disambiguate the phrase in the context in which it appears. In what follows, the scope of this chapter will be narrowed down to that of the quality of translated texts; for descriptions of quality assessment of translation processes, the reader is referred to, for instance, Mertin (2006) or Drugan (2013).

In order to avoid any further conceptual misunderstandings, it is also useful to clarify the difference between the two interpretations of the abbreviation *TQA*, since both are equally important to both the industry, including institutions, and research. Although the occurrence of the abbreviation *TQA* is fairly frequent, its meaning is not stable and may vary depending on the user. For some, it means translation quality *assessment*, the topic of the present chapter. For others, however, it refers to translation quality *assurance*, and is related to the translation process. The former interpretation establishes a link between TQA and the act of pronouncing a quality judgement about the translated text (like *travaux scénographiques*), while the latter sees TQA as the provision in a company's activities to take care of quality or its implementation, application and management of quality control. The industry group TAUS (Translation Automation User Society), which arguably may not reflect the view of translation scholars but aims at providing data services to both buyers and providers of language and translation services, defined translation quality assurance in their translation technology report as "a combination of technology and processes to prevent errors from creeping into translation projects" or the set of "procedures in the whole translation process (from initial order to final delivery and file closure)" (TAUS 2013: 22) in order to have the translation comply with standards that are recognized, such as the European norm EN 15038:2006 or the international standard ISO 17100:2015

[1]On the topic of translation manuals and style guides cf. Svoboda (2017 [this volume]).

(2015). Hence, such a set of procedures consists of an "ordered set of steps to guarantee quality" (TAUS 2013: 22) both prior, during, and after the translation, and even after the delivery of the translation. Translation quality assurance includes, for instance, the "decision process in translator assignment: which translator(s) are best match to the task, factoring in skill level, prior QA scores, availability and domain of expertise" (TAUS 2013: 22). Consequently, translation quality assurance both precedes and follows translation quality assessment. The assessment of translation quality, however, is in itself also ambiguous, since the term *translation* may, as is well-known, refer to either the product of translation or the process, whether the latter is to be found at a micro-level – in the translator's brain – or at a macro-level – all the other processes whether they are part of translation service provision, initiate a translation to be produced or whether they are set in motion by a particular translation in a particular community.

While the meaning of TQA may vary rather substantially, the concept of *quality* itself seems to be more stable and commonly agreed upon. Princeton University's Wordnet, whose large English lexical database also interlinks the senses of the words, defines *quality* as "an essential and distinguishing attribute of something or someone" (University 3.1, 2017). Some other definitions are suggested throughout this book, yet they do not diverge significantly. However, the word *quality* is mostly used in the sense of 'calibre', or, as the "degree or grade of excellence or worth" (WordNet 3.1 2017). Although this is a clear matter, there have been many debates about what exactly constitutes the 'calibre' of a text and many contributions to the topic have been produced by translation scholars, such as Lauscher (2000); Maier (2000); Lee-Jahnke (2001); Colina (2009); Van de Poel & Segers (2007) and Depraetere & Vackier (2011).

In spite of the terminological confusion, the above-mentioned scholars' findings and discussions were fruitful in that they have also brought a set of characteristics of translation quality assessment to the foreground and the present chapter will present the most prominent ones, discussing their conceptualization. This will be based on both the literature on translation quality and on translation quality practices in translation training, where teachers are experienced assessors of translations on a regular if not on a daily basis. Four main parameters have been distinguished which play a role in the assessment of the quality of a translation product. They are: purpose or functionality of the translation quality assessment, the translation quality level aimed at, the criteria including the weighting and scaling of the criteria, and actor performing the assessment.

In order to illustrate the parameters, data will be presented that were gathered in a pilot case study about the translation quality assessment of one institution as reported on in 2008. Following Schäffner et al. (2014: 493–494) in taking the label 'institutional translation' to refer to translating in or for a specific organisation, the translation practices by the Service central de traduction allemande (SCTA) may well be considered as institutional translation. The SCTA is the central translation service provider for German in Belgium since 1976, situated in Malmedy and part of the *Service public fédéral Intérieur* (abbreviated as SPF Intérieur, the Federal Public Service for Domestic Affairs), employing about 25 people for translation and coordination tasks. They translate federal laws adopted by the Belgian parliament into German as well as newsletters of the SPF Intérieur. They present their translations and terminological work in two databases, TRADUCTIONS and SEMAMDY respectively, both of which can be consulted on their website (SCTA n.d.).

2 Purpose of the translation quality assessment

The first parameter in a product translation quality assessment exercise is closely related to that of the object, i.e. it is the purpose of the translation product quality assessment. Although many translations may have been produced to an audience that is knowledgeable of the source language,[2] the purpose of many other translations is to be read – and in the context of institutional translation also to be relied upon – by somebody who is assumed not to know the language of a source text. The purpose of a translation quality assessment may vary considerably. Compare this, for instance, to a piece of clothing whose purpose is to be worn by somebody, and can therefore be tested to fulfil different purposes: will the piece of clothing make people warm enough in freezing temperatures or protect people from a blazing sun, will it support a certain part of the human body so the wearer does not suffer, will it make someone sexually attractive? Just like a piece of clothing can be tested, the quality of a translation can be tested with different intents: will the reader be attracted to buy a certain product, will the reader know what the important contents are of a product that has been bought, will the reader use the company's new machine or tool safely and efficiently, will the reader know what to do in certain life-threatening situations, will the reader understand the essential writing qualities of a foreign author, does a teacher find appropriate elements in students' translations so that their translation competence can be developed most smoothly, will a teacher allow a student to enter the market with a translation degree, or will a company hire an employee? There

[2] An example is the publication of scholarly materials in the target language following language policies that protect languages with a lesser diffusion.

is even one instance in which the translation assessment itself becomes a central point of focus and is even made public. This is the case with literary translation criticism expressed in reviews in newspapers, magazines or journals which may help readers decide whether they find the translation worth reading.

Other purpose features can be related to elements from the translation situation itself. As a resource centre for language and translation industries worldwide TAUS, for instance, identifies further criteria. They identify the purpose of a translation as to whether it will be used as audio/video material, for marketing or online help purposes, as training material or user documentation, for a user interface or as website content; they also distinguish between translations to be used in a regulated industry versus those that operate within those industries that are not regulated, whether the translation is to be read by company staff only or not, and whether the communication channel fulfills a Business-to-Business, Business-to-Consumer or Consumer-to-Consumer purpose (TAUS 2013).

When requested for more information on their quality assessment procedure, SCTA readily produced a workflow for their translation quality procedures with *two* revision and correction stages and their internal and external customer satisfaction surveys. Neither, however, revealed any explicit statements about the purpose of their translation product quality assessment. It is clear that they assume that any person interested will understand why the translation product needs to be assessed and revised twice.

3 Translation quality levels

Setting a certain translation quality level has the aim to allow a person to judge a translation unacceptable if it turns out to have lower quality. While many professional translators proclaimed and still proclaim that they aim at the highest possible level of translation quality, the machine translation industry seems to have changed market expectations profoundly. At present, there is a wide variety among translation level distinctions both in the industry and education, going from just one level to classifications which yield five and even considerably more different levels of translation quality.

A broad distinction has, for instance, been made by Williams (2004) between two main different quality levels in the industry. "*Revisable" quality* (after linguistic quality inspection, LQI) is the quality achieved after *proofreading*, i.e. after errors in translated texts have been identified and corrected in the areas of terminology, sentence level features such as spelling, punctuation, grammar (syntax, morphology), lexicon, textual level features like terminological consistency and contextual features like compliance with style guide. *"Publishable" quality*, in contrast, is produced after comparing the translation with source text, i.e. after identification and correction of mistranslations that are due to misinterpretation by unwarranted omissions, additions or changes. After such source text alignment, compliance with domain register and phraseology, stylistic consistency, and accuracy, usability and readability with regard to the specific target audience/end-user are assured. In Europe, this is often called revision / editing / review, although the terminology as used in the ISO 17100:2015 (2015) standard is slightly different and alignment does not need to precede review.

While referring to market practices in France, Gouadec distinguishes three levels: "(1) rough-cut, (2) fit-for-delivery (but still requiring minor improvements or not yet fit for its broadcast medium), and (3) fit-for-broadcast translation (accurate, efficient, and ergonomic)", recognizing the possibility of an intervening "'fit-for-revision' grade to describe translations that can be revised within a reasonable time at a reasonable cost" (Gouadec 2010). The distinction between the fit-for-delivery translation and the fit-for-revision translation seems vague, however, the former being formulated in terms of potential use and the latter in terms of time. The combination of those two different parameters allows for overlapping categories.

In education, students are ideally assessed like professionals. However, such expectations may well be unrealistic since students have not been able to build expertise over the years. In order to provide a fair system, different levels can be set up recognizing the pedagogical aims of the course and the items discussed in the course (see also Vandepitte forthcoming). Evaluation grids with various levels can be used to communicate criteria to students. A fair number of translation training programmes applies grids with different levels for academic purposes, but the EAGLES project at University of Geneva is an example in which four different quality levels in the industry have been recognized. Their *raw translations* convey the central meaning of the original text, but there will be grammatical errors and misspellings. Scientific abstracts often take that form. Secondly, the quality level of a *normal quality translation* is slightly higher since there are no grammatical errors. However, some passages may sound awkward. A typical example would be the translation of a technical manual. The next level of *extra-quality translation* means that the translation is also idiomatic and culturally assimilated to the target culture. Translations of advertisement brochure or literature would belong to this category. Finally, an *adaptation of an original text* does not need to correspond to the original and also omissions are acceptable (King et al. 1995). With its reference to different text types, this scaling is not related to any pedagogical aims but it introduces students to the translation jobs that trainees may well be liable to translate in their future professional lives.

In the case of SCTA's quality practice, neither their customer survey (Figure 1 in section 4) nor description of their quality assessment process mentions any explicit differentiation of quality levels. Nevertheless, there is a symbolic colouring of the three bands into which the points on the scale have been grouped in Figure 1 – with red for grades 1–4, orange for grades 5–7 and green for grades 8–10 – which may actually reveal the degree of acceptability of a grade. From this, it could also be assumed that their services will not aim at any levels of translation product quality lower than top quality.

4 Translation quality assessment criteria

At international level, agreement has been reached by the ISO on the following items that are also relevant in the quality assessment of a translation product: codes and representations of languages and countries (ISO 639-2:1998, ISO 639-1-2002, ISO 639-3:2007, ISO 2859-1), specialized vocabulary in the fields of micrographics, laboratory apparatus, heat treatments, shipbuilding, and so on, document formats ISO 8601:2004, information technology (ISO/IEC 10646:2014, ISO/IEC 646:1991), and computer applications in terminology (ISO 16642:2003).

These standards are all related to either vocabulary and terminology or formatting and technology. However, those areas are not the sole criteria to be assessed, and, as it happens, the translation market is rife with varying views on the number and the selection of other criteria that need to be taken into account in a translation assessment exercise. Many organizations, whether private, such as Lionbridge or Sajan, or public, have set up their own criteria, including a subset from the following set of criteria: faithfulness to the source text, grammar, syntax, spelling, punctuation, vocabulary, style, register, coherence, cohesion, and fluency.

Most of these are construed as *error* categories. An approach that does not focus on errors is Gouadec's description of four domains from which criteria can be taken to describe the translated text: the linguistic-stylistic-rhetorical-communicative domain, the factual-technical-semantic-cultural domain, the functional-ergonomic domain, and, finally, a 'domain', in which the translation is compared to the source text, taking into account any linguistic or cultural gaps and any intended changes in medium or audience "even to the point that there remains very little parallelism between the original and the end product of the translating process" (Gouadec 2010). Noteworthy, the lack of similarity between source and target texts reveal how broad Gouadec's approach is to be interpreted, since institutional translation would hardly ever find such differences acceptable, except perhaps for shorter, illustrative passages.

4.1 Scaling of the criteria

Like any other type of assessment, the quality of a translation in terms of a particular criterion can be decided on by assigning it a certain position on a scale going from low to high quality. Such scales would allow for comparison of different translations with each other. However, quality grades are not often made explicit as such in specifications. They mainly seem to appear in education, where translations need to be marked and marks will produce a ranking among students. Obviously, standards like the ISO 17100:2015, which are process-oriented, will not include scaling either. Nevertheless, most assessment criteria do allow for grading, and some companies' and/or institutions' assessments are operating with systems of scaled grades for quality criteria (see e.g. Strandvik, Strandvik 2017 [this volume]), some of which are even fairly complex.

A simple example can be seen in the satisfaction survey distributed by the SCTA (2015). Figure 1 (§6) shows how the quality has been given 10 points on a scale which allows customers to assess according to a system that they have been used to in school. The combination of three criteria in one question, however, does not allow them to make distinctions and may result in average quality scores that will not reveal any problematic areas.

4.2 Weighting of the criteria

Finally, organizations also determine the value of each criterion vis-à-vis the other criteria. Depending on the settings of other parameters, and, in particular, that of the purpose of the assessment, certain aspects will carry more weight in the assessment than others. Such relative importance of the criteria components to each other can be visualized in, for example, a pie-chart.

5 Actors involved in the translation quality assessment

The final aspect to be discussed is the actors involved in the translation quality assessment. Although arguably actors may be seen as a major aspect in a *process*, their impact on the assessment of the translation product is not to be underestimated and gives them a place in this survey of translation product criteria, too. Depending on the purpose of the quality assessment, certain actors will need to be involved in carrying out the translation quality assessment. As may already have become clear from the preceding paragraphs, various actors may be involved in TQA.

On the one hand, there are people that set standards for translation quality, and, on the other hand, there are people that carry out the tests. In many cases, the two acts are carried out by the same person. There are *standard-setters* at individual level (teachers in translation training, for instance) or at organizational level. In the translation context, the latter usually operate at international level. One such standard-setter for translation services was the European Committee for Standardization CEN in collaboration with the European Union of Associations of Translation Agencies, producing the European Standard EN 15038:2006 . This standard was later replaced by the ISO 17100:2015 (2015) by the International Organization for Standardization (ISO 17100:2015), the worldwide federation of national standards bodies. The latter organization carries out preparatory work in technical committees, in which each member body interested in a particular committee can be represented. Sometimes other international organizations, governmental and non-governmental, are also involved. Draft International Standards adopted by the technical committees are approved when three quarters of the member bodies agree. Some more private initiatives are also taken: an example is SAE International, a global association of engineers and technical experts in the aerospace, automotive and commercial-vehicle industries. They produced a *translation quality metric* called SAE J2450_201608, which is "applicable to translations of automotive service information into any target language. The metric may be applied regardless of the source language or the method of translation (i.e., human translation, computer assisted translation or machine translation)" (SAE, 2016[3]), except for texts, the style of which is also important (e.g., owner's manuals or marketing literature). The metric, which acquired the status of a standard in the first decade of the twenty-first century, is assumed to provide for a more objective assessment of translations in the automotive industry.

Testing the quality of a translation can be carried out by "translators, executives, quality managers, heads of departments, project managers, clients, editors, revisers, terminologists, software engineers and sales and marketing staff" alike (Drugan 2013: 3). But other actors may also be involved: translation scholars have their own individual systems, sometimes moderated by some element of intersubjectivity when a few more testers are involved in the rating of translations or when audiences of subtitles are consulted (Delia 2014). End-users as translation audiences are also sometimes consulted in the commercial world: buyers of

[3]http://standards.sae.org/j2450_201608

products may bring to bear on the quality of a translation, by way of customer satisfaction surveys, usability testing (for instructive types of text, for instance) and TAUS's Dynamic Quality Framework (DQF).

Customer satisfaction surveys are actually also employed by the SCTA. Figure 1 below shows their question about the translation product quality and culd be translated into English as Are the translations delivered faithful, of good readability and coherent?:

Qualité										
Les traductions fournies sont-elles fiables, d'une bonne lisibilité et cohérentes ?	10	9	8	7	6	5	4	3	2	1
Commentaires/Suggestions										

Figure 1: Extract from SCTA internal/external customer satisfaction survey (SCTA 2015)

The question put to SCTA customers immediately reveals its three main criteria: adequacy (*fiables*), and two features of acceptability, i.e. readability (*d'une bonne lisibilité*) and coherence (*cohérentes*).

The TAUS DQF was first established in 2012, undergoes regular updates and allows buyers of translations to decide on the type of quality test necessary to apply to the translation product which they have bought. The DQF requests its users to decide on the settings of parameters. The parameters available are content category, regulated industry, internal communication and channel, and on the basis of the user's settings, the DQF will automatically suggest one evaluation model among various evaluation models (error typology, adequacy/fluency and readability evaluation, for instance) and it will also perform an automated evaluation metric (TAUS 2017).

In order to avoid what the industry considers to be costly human labour in the translation quality assessment process, it is also looking for automated testing by means of software tools. A comparison of the performance of such tools can be found in Debove et al. (2011), and the formal quality check performance of one such tool (QA Distiller) was tested by Depraetere & Vackier (2011) on Spanish into French student translations by comparing it with human measurements, investigating its degree of indicativeness of overall quality.

Summing up the discussion above, the parameters in translation quality assessment can be presented as in Table 1.

Table 1: . Parameters in translation quality assessment

Object
process
product
service

Purpose
sell the translation
sell another product
recommend (or not) a translation to the general public
hire an employee
grade a student
develop a student's translation competences, ...

Actor
producer of translation quality: translator, whether a professional, an amateur or a student
producer of certain translation norms: ISO (EN and national norm-giving institutions)
quality testers: client / commissioner / employer in the professional field who expects a certain standard, trainer who expects a certain standard from a student, researcher into translation quality...

TQA-level aimed at
1-level: so-called 100% quality
2-level: e.g. revisable versus publishable quality
3-level: e.g. green, orange and red bands
more than 3 levels

Criteria involved in the product assessment
alignment with the source text
style
terminology
grammar
syntax
spelling
punctuation
vocabulary
register
coherence
cohesion
fluency, ...

Scaling of criteria
measures used to identify the quality of the translation in terms of each criterion
Weighting of criteria
relative importance of the criteria

6 Summary and conclusion

This chapter has presented the following factors of translation quality assessment: its object, its purpose, the actors involved, the TQA-level aimed at, the criteria relevant to theassessment, their scaling and any weighting.

While this summary may not include all potential variants of parameter settings, nor even all parameters themselves, the survey aims at presenting a clearer idea of the issue of translation product quality assessment and facilitating discussion of the topic among different stakeholders.

Whether this survey is practically applicable to all types of translation products is something which future practice only will tell. The set of parameters as outlined above may certainly be helpful in cases where the assessment of a translation product turns out to be of the utmost importance, which is typical of institutional translation.

The description of SCTA's translation product assessment has shown that its public statements do not contain much explicit information. In order to improve the visibility of the work involved in translation, however, more informative statements about the purpose of the assessment, the criteria assessed or the quality level aimed at would be welcome.

References

BBC-News. 2008. *30 October 2008. E-mail error ends up on road sign.* http://news.bbc.co.uk/2/hi/7702913.stm.

Colina, Sonia. 2009. Further evidence for a functionalist approach to translation quality evaluation. *Target* 21(2). 235–264. DOI:10.1075/target.21.2.02col

Debove, Antonia, Sabrina Furlan & Ilse Depraetere. 2011. A contrastive analysis of five automated QA tools (QA Distiller 6.5.8, Xbench 2.8, ErrorSpy 5.0, SDL Trados 2007 QA Checker 2.0 and SDLX 2007 SP2 QA Check). In Ilse Depraetere (ed.), *Perspectives on translation quality*, 161–192. Berlin: de Gruyter Mouton.

Delia, Chiaro. 2014. The eyes and ears of the beholder? Translation, humor and perception. In Dror Abend-David (ed.), *Media and translation. An interdisciplinary approach*, 197–219. New York: Bloomsbury Academic.

Depraetere, Ilse & Thomas Vackier. 2011. Comparing formal translation evaluation and meaning-oriented translation evaluation: or how QA tools can(not) help. In Ilse Depraetere (ed.), *Perspectives on translation quality*, 25–50. Berlin: de Gruyter Mouton.

Drugan, Joanna. 2013. *Quality in professional translation: assessment and improvement.* London: Bloomsbury.

Gouadec, Daniel. 2010. Quality in translation. In Yves Gambier & van Doorslaer Luc (eds.), *Handbook of Translation Studies*, vol. 1, 270–275. Amsterdam: John Benjamins.

ISO 16642:2003. 2003. *Computer applications in terminology – Terminological markup framework*. Geneva: ISO. http://www.iso.org/standard/32347.html.

ISO 17100:2015. 2015. *Translation services – Requirements for translation services*. Geneva: ISO. http://www.iso.org/iso/catalogue_detail.htm?csnumber=59149.

ISO 2859-1. 2006. *Sampling procedures. Part 1: Sampling schemes indexed by acceptable quality limit (AQL) for lot-by-lot inspection*. Geneva: ISO.

ISO 639-1-2002. 2013. *Codes for the representation of names of languages – Part 1: Alpha-2 code*. Geneva: ISO. https://www.iso.org/standard/22109.html.

ISO 639-2:1998. 2016. *Codes for the representation of names of languages – Part 2: Alpha-3 code*. Geneva. https://www.iso.org/standard/4767.html.

ISO 639-3:2007. 2016. *Codes for the representation of names of languages – Part 3: Alpha-3 code for comprehensive coverage of languages*. Geneva: ISO. https://www.iso.org/standard/39534.html.

ISO 8601:2004. 2004. *Data elements and interchange formats – Information interchange – Representation of dates and times*. Geneva: ISO. http://www.iso.org/standard/40874.html.

ISO/IEC 10646:2014. 2014. *Information technology – universal coded character set (ucs)*. Geneva: ISO. https://www.iso.org/standard/63182.html, accessed 2017-9-30.

ISO/IEC 646:1991. 1991. *Information technology – ISO 7-bit coded character set for information interchange*. Geneva: ISO. http://www.iso.org/standard/4777.html, accessed 2017-9-30.

King, Maghi, Bente Maegaard & Jörg Schütz. 1995. *Translation quality. EAGLES. Evaluation of natural language processing systems. Final report. EAGLES DOCUMENT EAG-EWG-PR.2*. http://www.issco.unige.ch/en/research/projects/ewg95//node165.html.

Lauscher, Susanne. 2000. Translation quality assessment. Where can theory and practice meet? *The Translator* 6(2). 149–168.

Lee-Jahnke, Hannelore. 2001. Aspects pédagogiques de l'évaluation des traductions. *Meta* 46(2). 258–271.

Maier, Carol. 2000. Introduction. *The Translator* 6(2). 137–148.

Mertin, Elvira. 2006. *Prozessorientiertes Qualitätsmanagement im Dienstleistungsbereich Übersetzen*. Leipzig: Peter Lang.

Schäffner, Christina, Luciana Sabina Tcaciuc & Wine Tesseur. 2014. Translation practices in political institutions: a comparison of national, supranational, and non-governmental organisations. *Perspectives. Studies in Translatology* 22(4). 493–510. DOI:10.1080/0907676X.2014.948890

SCTA. 2015. *Appréciation des prestations fournies*. Unpublished internal document.

SCTA. n.d. *Qui sommes nous?* http://www.scta.be/Wer-wir-sind/Wer-wir-sind.aspx, accessed 2017-9-30.

for Standardization (CEN), European Committee. 2006. *EN 15038:2006 Translation services – service requirements*. Brussels: CEN.

Strandvik, Ingemar. 2015. On quality in EU multilingual lawmaking. In Susan Šarčević (ed.), *Language and culture in EU Law. Multidisciplinary perspectives*, 141–165. Farnham: Ashgate.

Strandvik, Ingemar. 2017. Evaluation of outsourced translations. State of play in the European Commission's Directorate-General for Translation (DGT). In Tomáš Svoboda, Łucja Biel & Krzysztof Łoboda (eds.), *Quality aspects in institutional translation* (Translation and Multilingual Natural Language Processing 8), 123–137. Berlin: Language Science Press. DOI:10.5281/zenodo.1048194

Svoboda, Tomáš. 2017. Translation manuals and style guides as quality assurance indicators: The case of the European Commission's Directorate-General for Translation. In Tomáš Svoboda, Łucja Biel & Krzysztof Łoboda (eds.), *Quality aspects in institutional translation* (Translation and Multilingual Natural Language Processing 8), 75–107. Berlin: Language Science Press. DOI:10.5281/zenodo.1048190

TAUS. 2013. *Quality assurance*. https//www.taus.net/file-downloads/download-file%3Fpath%3DTOC%25252F370-taus-translation-technology-landscape-table-of-contents.pdf.

TAUS. 2015. *Dynamic Quality Framework report 2015*. http://www.taus.net/think-tank/reports/evaluate-reports/dynamic-quality-framework-report-2015.

TAUS. 2017. *Quality Dashboard. Measuring and Benchmarking Translation Quality*. https://www.taus.net/quality-dashboard-lp, accessed 2017-9-30.

University, Princeton. 2010. *About WordNet*. http://wordnet.princeton.edu.

Van de Poel, Chris & Winibert Segers (eds.). 2007. *De ijkpuntenmethode: perspectieven, beperkingen, verder onderzoek*. Leuven: Acco.

Vandepitte, Sonia. Forthcoming. Teaching professional standards and quality assurance in translation. In Monika Krein-Kühle, Barbara Ahrens, Ursula Wienen, Michael Schreiber & Silvia Hansen-Schirra (eds.). Berlin: Frank & Timme.

Williams, Malcolm. 2004. *Translation quality assessment: an argumentation-centred approach*. Ottawa: Ottawa University Press.

Chapter 3

Quality in institutional EU translation: Parameters, policies and practices

Łucja Biel
University of Warsaw

Over the last decade EU institutions have raised the profile of quality, as evidenced by an increased number of translation policies and guidelines. The objective of the chapter is to identify the quality parameters of EU translation by synthesizing and evaluating institutional policies and practices on the one hand and the academic literature on the other hand. Two interrelated dimensions will be distinguished: (a) the quality of translation at the textual level and (b) the quality of processes in translation service provision. The former covers two subdimensions – equivalence and textual fit/clarity while the latter covers the management of people, processes and resources, as well as the availability of translations. One of the promising developments is the reframing of quality discourse by the explicit linking of translation quality at the textual level to genre clusters, with a shift of focus from equivalence to clarity. On the other hand, such classifications may be seen as being triggered by the need to prioritize documents, as part of the fit-for-purpose approach, in order to prudently manage resources and costs in line with the required level of quality.

Translation has been at the core of the European integration, being its key enabler and facilitator from the very beginnings of the European Coal and Steel Community in the early 1950s. Because of the significance and scale of European Union (EU) translation, its quality is a fundamental concept, which has gained increased attention in EU institutional policies, increasingly so in the last decade. Challenging some fundamental concepts of Translation Studies, such as the source text, target text, translation process, etc. (cf. Biel 2014: 59ff), EU translation also challenges our understanding of translation quality. As emphasized by Dollerup (2001), the quality of EU translation tends to be evaluated "by criteria which do not really apply" (285) and "it is not translation alone that makes the product" (290), but a complex array of political, ideological and procedural

Łucja Biel. 2017. Quality in institutional EU translation: Parameters, policies and practices. In Tomáš Svoboda, Łucja Biel & Krzysztof Łoboda (eds.), *Quality aspects in institutional translation*, 31–57. Berlin: Language Science Press. DOI:10.5281/zenodo.1048183

factors. The objective of this chapter is to identify the quality parameters of EU translation by critically analyzing institutional policies and practices and by synthesizing the existing literature and viewpoints from within EU institutions and from the outside. The chapter will first define and categorize EU translation, map quality in the EU context and its components, making a fundamental distinction between the quality of translation as a product and quality of processes in translation service provision. Finally, the chapter will identify key threats and challenges to quality.

1 Mapping the field – what is EU translation?

EU translation is a multi-faceted, broad and fuzzy category which may be defined as translation rendered by and for European Union institutions. In the most prototypical sense, it is translation provided in-house by the translation services of EU institutions. However, EU translation also covers translations outsourced to external contractors and paid for and, to some extent, controlled by EU institutions.

As a consequence of having institutions as agents/commissioning entities, EU translation is naturally placed in a broader superordinate category of INSTITUTIONAL translation. Institutional translation is described as self-translation because translation is institutions' means of communication with the outside world and, hence, "the institution itself gets translated" (Koskinen 2008: 22). Since institutions regulate and control behaviour, monitor compliance, and create a shared cognitive background (Scott, quoted in Koskinen 2008: 18), institutional translation is affected by institutional norms (Koskinen 2000: 50; Wagner et al. 2002: 65; Felici 2010: 101), institutional patterns of behaviour (Kang 2011: 144), and the institutional culture of translating (Mason 2004 [2003]: 470).

By extension, and in view of the fact that the European Union is a supranational political union, EU translation may also be classified as POLITICAL translation (cf. Trosborg 1997: 147) or even narrower as diplomatic translation because many EU documents are a result of complex delicate negotiations and political compromise between the Member States.[1]

EU translation may also be defined through genres or text types which are translated. EU translation is often perceived stereotypically as legal translation. While legal translation, i.e. the translation of EU legislation and case law, is a special constituent *category* of EU translation which is critically central to the func-

[1] See Šarčević (2007: 44) on EU law as *droit diplomatique* for the same reason.

tioning of the European Union, it comprises a salient (and by no means silent) minority of documents translated by EU translation services. EU translation is diverse and covers a continuum from expert-to-expert to expert-to-lay communication (cf. Biel 2014: 56). In addition to law, specialized (expert-to-expert) genres include official communications, institutional reports, minutes, and international agreements, whereby institutions communicate with experts, such as national governments and MEPs. In expert-to-lay communication institutions communicate with the general public, e.g. citizens, through such genres as booklets, letters to citizens, press releases, as well as multimodal genres, such as institutional websites or tweets.

2 Translation quality as a scalar and dynamic concept

One of the well-known definitions of quality, borrowed from marketing, is the degree to which a product or service meets clients' needs, expectations and specifications (Kotler & Lane Keller 2006: 146–148). This view is also valid in the context of translation,[2] where the quality of translated texts is perceived as a gradable rather than a (good-bad) binary concept (cf. Biel 2011a: 15). The perception of quality has recently evolved[3] in Translation Studies, especially with the advent of machine translation and crowdsourcing (cf. Jiménez-Crespo 2017), shifting from the negative approach of error counting to the evaluation of translation against readers' expectations, intended purpose and other communicative factors (Colina 2009: 238; see also Vandepitte 2017, an introductory chapter to this book, which discusses quality-related concepts in more depth). Quality has been reconceptualized as a dynamic negotiated concept which comprises varied degrees of quality, depending on a number of factors, including fitness for purpose, utility, time, and price (cf. Jiménez-Crespo 2017: 478, 482). This understanding of quality is also evident in industry standards, e.g. ISO 17100:2015 and EN 15038:2006 , which see quality of translations as suitability for the agreed purpose (cf. Biel 2011b). The dynamism and relativity of the concept of quality are also evident in its varied perception and understanding among stakeholders, e.g. translators, requesters, end users, due to their different expectations and needs (cf. Strandvik 2015: 142–143). Key dimensions of translation quality will be discussed in the next section.

[2]For a comprehensive overview of theoretical and professional approaches to quality see e.g. Drugan (2013) and House (2015).

[3]See also Prieto Ramos (2015) for a detailed discussion of quality models in legal translation.

3 Quality of EU translation

Thus, the concept of quality is multidimensional and I propose in the context of institutional EU translation to distinguish two interrelated and overlapping dimensions: the quality of translation at the textual level with TRANSLATION VIEWED AS A PRODUCT and the quality of processes in translation service provision with TRANSLATION VIEWED AS A SERVICE. The former covers two subdimensions – equivalence and textual fit/clarity while the latter covers the management of people, processes and resources. It should be noted that the quality of translation service provision strongly affects the quality of translation products.

3.1 Quality of EU translation at the textual level: translation as a product

As aptly observed by Strandvik (2015: 142), quality is "the sum of a number of different quality characteristics which may need to be ranked in order of priority or may even be contradictory". Such quality characteristics are well visible, inter alia, in the European Commission's specifications addressed to potential external translators: "[translations] can be used as they stand upon delivery, without any further formatting, revision, review and/or correction",[4] which is phrased in terms of accuracy consistency and clarity:

- "complete" (no omissions or additions)
- "accurate and consistent rendering of the source text"
- correct references to any already published documents
- internal terminological consistency and consistency with reference materials
- clarity, relevant register and observance of text-type conventions
- no language errors and correct formatting
- compliance with instructions.[5]

[4]Omnibus, Tender Specification, p. 8, https://infoeuropa.eurocid.pt/files/database/000064001-000065000/000064078_2.pdf (Accessed 2017-07-01).

[5]Omnibus, op. cit., p. 8–9.

It is worth noting that compared to 2008,[6] the word *faithful* disappeared from the descriptors of quality targeted at external contractors. The above list may be regarded as a set of characteristics to be possessed by a high-quality translation in the EU context (see Hanzl & Beaven 2017 [this volume] for a similar set of descriptors at the Council).

The quality of EU translation products is posited here, with some adaptations after Chesterman (2004) and Biel (2011b; 2014), to comprise the following fundamental variables:

- Dimension 1: **Equivalence** of translation in relation to the source text (fidelity, accuracy of information transfer), in relation to other language versions (multilingual concordance) and in terms of **consistency/continuity** with preceding and/or higher-ranking texts,
- Dimension 2: **Textual fit** (naturalness) of translation in relation to corresponding non-translated texts produced in the Member States, as well as the interrelated concept of **clarity** (readability) of translation.

I will illustrate below how these two dimensions are prioritized in the EU institutions' translation policies and practices.

As a result of a more dire need to balance translation costs, demand and quality triggered after the last waves of accessions, recent years have observed an intensification of documents on translation quality coupled with a substantial renarration of translation quality discourse in EU institutions, in particular in the European Commission and the Council. The new narrative has downplayed faithfulness (that is the equivalence dimension) as the key characteristics of high-quality translation by reorientation towards more functional categories of FITNESS FOR PURPOSE, with occasional explicit references to ISO 17100:2015 (e.g. DGT 2015: 3), and consequently by linking quality requirements to genres grouped into a number of clusters (I will refer to it as the genre-based approach; however, it should be borne in mind that EU institutions do not frame it as such), which has put the concept of CLARITY to the fore (dimension 2). This reworking of the concept of quality should be evaluated as a proactive move which prioritizes relevant characteristics of quality, depending on a communicative purpose behind a genre, rather than relying on a stereotyped perception of EU translation as legal only. It is worth stressing that the new approach is in line with the prominence of the concept of genre in Translation Studies (cf. Biel 2017)

[6]Cf. "the target text is a faithful, accurate and consistent translation of the source text" (DGT 2008: 6).

EU institutions have attempted to classify documents to prioritize their translation and revision for more than a decade (cf. Court of Auditors' report 2006); however, recent years have brought more pronounced narratives linking quality levels with document types. This is especially visible in the European Commission's DGT, which evolved "towards a more conscious, structured and systematic approach to quality assurance" (Strandvik (2017b: 52)). Its quality advisers drafted a document called *DGT Translation Quality Guidelines* in 2015, followed by a summary version for external contractors *Translation Quality Info Sheets for Contractors* in 2017, where they introduce four categories of texts and link quality requirements and control to genre clusters and risks (see also Strandvik 2017b):

- Category A: Legal acts;
  - EU legal acts;
  - documents used in administrative or legal proceedings and inquiries;
  - documents for procurement or funding programmes, tenders, grants applications, contracts;
  - recruitment notices, EPSO (European Personnel Selection Office) competition notices and test documents;
- Category B: Policy and administrative documents
  - accompanying documents not formally part of legal acts;
  - white and green papers;
  - other official administrative documents, e.g. budget, reports, guidelines.
- Category C: Information for the public
  - press releases, memos;
  - articles to be published in the press, speeches, interviews;
  - leaflets, brochures, posters;
  - web texts.
- Category D: Input for EU legislation, policy formulation and administration – eight subcategories of incoming documents from Member States, other stakeholders, citizens and non-EU countries and external bodies.

The highest quality is expected of Category A and within this genre cluster – of multilingual legislation. Quality descriptors foreground the equivalence dimension ("legal accuracy", DGT 2016b: 6) to ensure uniform interpretation and application (cf. Šarčević 1997: 72) and the same result in all the official languages (cf. Pozzo 2012: 1191), which is also referred to as "multilingual concordance" (DGT 2016b: 4) and the "horizontal dimension" (Robertson 2015: 44). In the context of multilingual law, equivalence relations are highly intertextual and complex — equivalence is presumed to exist between all language versions of a legal instrument, i.e. between the original and the target text, but also between translations into other languages. Equivalence is "proclaimed" (Hermans 2007: 11) as "an a priori characteristic" of EU translation (Koskinen 2000: 49) — it is "existential equivalence" (Koskinen 2000: 51) and "mandatory legal equivalence" (Tosi 2002: 180–181) due to the fact that all the language versions are presumed to have the same legal value regardless of whether or not they are equivalent as to their meaning (cf. Tosi 2002: 180). This presumption is known as the principle of equal authenticity (Šarčević 1997: 64) and the principle of plurilinguistic equality (van Els 2001). The quality of multilingual legislation is also required, to a lesser degree, to take into account the textual fit and clarity dimension. Clear language[7] and language quality are explicitly mentioned as quality requirements with reference to legislation (cf. DGT 2016b: 6). They are to ensure its accessibility, predictability and legal certainty (Strandvik 2015: 146). As pointed out by Strandvik, there is a general consensus among the legal services of EU institutions that "all language versions of a piece of legislation should *deviate as little as possible* from the target cultures' drafting conventions" (2015: 153, emphasis added). On the other hand, DGT Translation Quality Guidelines admit that there is "only limited leeway for 'localising' Category A" to target language (TL) conventions (DGT 2016b: 14). Furthermore, it should be pointed out that the requirement of minimum deviations from TL conventions may be difficult to satisfy due to the high hybridity of EU language. The hybridity results from a number of factors, such as the complex multilingual multi-stage drafting process intertwined with translation (Doczekalska 2009: 360), fusion of languages and the frequent involvement of non-native speakers (Wagner et al. 2002: 76), cultural neutralisation and hybridity of texts, unstable source texts (Stefaniak 2013), quality of drafting (Tosi 2002: 184, Šarčević & Robertson 2013: 22), preference for literal translation techniques (Koskinen 2000: 54), as well as distortions typical of the translation process (cf. Biel 2014 for a detailed discussion). As a result, EU

[7] *Legislative Drafting. A Commission Manual* goes as far as to include "reader-friendliness" in the legislative checklist (European Commission 1997: 78).

legislation has led to the emergence of distinct legal varieties of national legal languages (cf. Biel 2014 and the Eurolect Observatory project[8]).

The highest clarity and textual fit requirements are set for Category C which comprises mainly informative texts addressed to the general public and EU citizens, representing expert-to-lay communication. Clarity is linked to the political objective of increasing the EU citizens' confidence in the European Union, enhancing its positive image and creating more interest in EU matters (cf. DGT 2015: 1, 12). Quality is achieved through the high localization of translations to target language conventions, avoidance of jargon, naturalness and idiomaticity of translations: "a key quality *desideratum* is to produce texts that read like originals in all languages" (DGT 2015: 2, 13). Translators have more freedom and are expected to provide translations which will function seamlessly in the target culture.

Categories B and D are between these two extremes – they place more focus on accuracy than Category C but more focus on naturalness than Category A.

Quality indicators for translation products, which are connected with ex-post quality monitoring (cf. Hanzl & Beaven 2017 [this volume] with reference to the Council) and control, are explicitly linked to errors and the CORRECTION RATE expressed through the number of corrigenda with the tolerance level set at < 0.5%, which is defined as:

- the ratio between the number of translations formally corrected during one year and the number of translations of the same year and the preceding two years that can be subject to such corrections (DGT 2016a: 4, footnote 4).

The most critical type of error in the EU context is an error in EU legislation which leads to a different, unintended regulation of rights and duties of private and public entities in the Member States (Kapko 2005: 2). Critical errors and corrigenda (cf. Bobek 2009) are usually connected with inappropriate information transfer, that is dimension 1 (equivalence, accuracy). It is also worth noting that, on the other hand, the descriptors of errors in the Commission have shifted from changes in information transfer (dimension 1) to impairment of product usability (dimension 2) (see Strandvik 2017a [this volume]).

To sum up, the fitness-for-purpose approach combined with the genre-based categorization of documents emphasize the cost-effective gradability of quality.

[8]More information: http://www.unint.eu/en/research/research-groups/39-higher-education/490-eurolect-observatory-interlingual-and-intralingual-analysis-of-legal-varieties-in-the-eu-setting.html (Accessed 2017-07-01).

On the one hand, they allow the institutions to manage their resources depending on the required level of quality – "very good" or "good enough": as observed by Martin, "the fit-for-purpose principle is an invaluable yardstick against which to balance risks and resources" (2007: 60). On the other hand, they have contributed to foregrounding often overlooked characteristics in the EU context, such as naturalness and clarity.

3.2 Quality of processes in EU translation service provision: translation as a service

The conceptualization of quality of translations through service provision rather than products is linked with market standards, such as ISO 17100:2015 and EN 15038:2006 , and is part of quality assurance. The key characteristics of service provision are proposed in the EU context to cover:

- a prerequisite – availability of translations in EU citizens' native languages,
- workflow management,
- people,
- translation resources (tools).

3.2.1 Availability of translations as a *sine qua non* condition: multilingualism and the selective translation policy

The *sine qua non* condition for discussing the quality of translation as a service is the availability of translations in official languages, in particular the availability to EU citizens in their native language. This prerequisite stems from one of the EU's fundamental values protected in its primary legislation – respect for linguistic diversity,[9] and the resulting multilingualism policy which is intended to give citizens access to EU legislation and information in their native languages as long as they have the status of an official language. Above all, the multilingualism policy imposes an obligation to publish the Official Journal of the European Union in all the official languages, and in particular to ensure that regulations and "documents of general application" are available in all the official languages.[10] The multilingualism policy also enables Member States or citizens to write to EU

[9] Article 3, Treaty on European Union (TEU), OJ C 326, 26.10.2012.

[10] Articles 5 and 6, Council Regulation No 1 determining the languages to be used by the European Economic Community, OJ 17, 6.10.1958.

institutions and receive a reply in one of the official languages and requires EU institutions to write to Member States and citizens in an official language of such a state/citizen.[11]

Currently, the EU multilingualism covers 24 official languages which are presumed to enjoy an equal status: Bulgarian, Croatian, Czech, Danish, Dutch, English, Estonian, Finnish, French, German, Greek, Hungarian, Irish, Italian, Latvian, Lithuanian, Maltese, Polish, Portuguese, Romanian, Slovak, Slovenian, Spanish and Swedish. Firstly, it should be noted that while the impressive scale of EU multilingualism includes speakers of 24 official languages, it does not include over 60 regional or minority languages and some co-official languages (e.g. Basque, Catalan, Welsh).[12] Secondly, the presumption of the equal status of all the official languages is limited to the legal validity and authenticity of the EU-wide legislation translated into such languages. Furthermore, some languages formally enjoy a privileged status of procedural languages (as "members of an elite club" (Craith 2006: 560) – English, French and German, and/or a status of pivot languages for relay translation, e.g. in the Court of Justice – French, English, German, Spanish and Italian.[13] Starting with the accession of Scandinavian countries in 1995 and strengthened after the 2004 enlargement, English replaced French as the dominant procedural language in most EU institutions (a notable exception being the Court of Justice with French as the procedural language) and became the lingua franca of the European Union. As a result, most documents are drafted in English and are selectively translated into other official languages. The main reason for the selective policy is the allocation of insufficient funds by the EU Budgetary Authorities (i.e. the Council and the Parliament) to ensure translation into all official languages,[14] as well as the increase in demand for translation in the last decade combined with the pressure on staff reductions in some institutions, which altogether evoke a strong need to prioritize categories of documents for translation (cf. DGT: 4) and introduce structural demand-reducing measures (cf. Strandvik 2017b).

This selective translation policy affects the availability of EU translations to citizens whose languages are underprivileged. As observed above, Council Regula-

[11]Articles 2 and 3, Council Regulation No 1, op. cit.

[12]https://europa.eu/european-union/topics/multilingualism_en (Accessed 2017-07-01).

[13]It also extends to the preference of selected – mainly procedural - languages in some EU agencies. For example, the European Union Intellectual Property Office (EUIPO) has 5 "working languages": English, French, German, Italian and Spanish.

[14]Decision of the European Ombudsman on complaint 3191/2006/(SAB)MHZ against the European Commission, https://www.ombudsman.europa.eu/en/cases/decision.faces/en/3248/html.bookmark (Accessed 2017-07-01).

tion No. 1 of 1958 imposes an obligation to ensure that "documents of general application" are available in all the official languages. Yet this seemingly broad term is in practice interpreted quite narrowly to comprise other types of secondary legislation (in particular directives, some decisions), as well as case law and a few selected document types. This is a compromise between demand, resources and costs, especially after the 2000s enlargements. The selective translation policy is referred to by the European Parliament itself as "controlled full multilingualism"[15] or "a pragmatic approach".[16] According to this policy full translation and interpreting applies only to the Parliament's official documents and plenary sessions, while preparatory documents are translated only into languages which are actually needed. A similar policy is pursued by the European Commission, whereby legislation and key political documents are translated into all EU official languages, as well as general information on its EUROPA website, with the rationale being a legal requirement or "serious disadvantage". Other documents are often translated into procedural language(s) only or those languages which are specifically needed – this applies in particular to correspondence with Member States or citizens, specialist information (technical information, campaigns, blogs, speeches, funding for research), news and urgent or "short-lived" information.[17] The (limited) choice of languages is framed as "evidence-based" to be balanced with importance, cost-effectiveness, limited budget and human resources for translation.[18] Obviously, this policy limits access to institutional information to speakers who do not know English and/or other procedural languages. The pragmatic approach is also adopted in the third largest EU institution – the Council. Its Language Service translates "almost all" legislation and "many major" policy documents into all official languages, admitting that "for efficiency's sake" about 70% of the Council's total pages are not translated at all as "for practical purposes" the Working Parties tend to work on a text drafted in one language (GSC 2012: 8).

[15]Cf. Article 1.2 of the European Parliament's *Code of Conduct on Multilingualism* of 16.06.2014: "The resources to be devoted to multilingualism shall be CONTROLLED by means of management on the basis of users' real needs, measures to make users more aware of their responsibilities and more effective planning of requests for language facilities." http://www.europarl.europa.eu/pdf/multilinguisme/coc2014_en.pdf (Accessed 2017-07-01).

[16]http://www.europarl.europa.eu/sides/getDoc.do?pubRef=-//EP//TEXTIM-PRESS20071017FCS118160DOCXMLV0//EN (Accessed 2017-07-01).

[17]http://ec.europa.eu/ipg/content/multilingualism/index_en.htm. See also the 2006 *Communication to the Commission* for an early categorization of texts into groups which may be outsourced (https://ec.europa.eu/transparency/regdoc/rep/2/2006/EN/2-2006-1489-EN-F1-1.Pdf) (Accessed 2017-07-01).

[18]http://ec.europa.eu/ipg/content/multilingualism/index_en.htm, https://europa.eu/european-union/abouteuropa/language-policy_en (Accessed 2017-07-01).

This pragmatic language regime has been referred to critically by Krzyżanowski & Wodak (2011) as hegemonic multilingualism which may suppress national languages and disempower certain nations. Mattila (2013: 33) goes even further and argues that the overuse of English as the main procedural language is indicative of unilingualism: "Despite the ideology underlining the multilingual character of the Union, one could speak of a development in the direction of unilingualism". Overall, the pragmatic approach, framed in the narrative of multilingualism and respect for linguistic diversity, reflects institutional policies connected with the realistic management of budgetary and human resources.

3.2.2 Quality of workflow management

The superordinate factor controlling the quality of translation as a service is workflow management – namely, how the provision of a translation service is managed against available resources. It ultimately contributes as a decisive factor to the quality of translation as a product. Management fundamentally affects the recruitment and allocation of human resources and the development of technical resources in light of budgetary constraints. It is also important for consistency of approach and for consistency of quality across and within institutions (cf. Drugan et al. 2018).

At a more global level, quality can be affected by the organizational structure of the translation service which prioritizes roles covering various aspects of quality assurance. It can be illustrated with the organization of the Directorate-General for Translation at the European Commission. As its organizational chart shows,[19] it is divided into six directorates, four of which (Directorates A to D) are in charge of Translation, including Directorate D which deals with procedural languages only, while the other two Directorate R is in charge of Resources and Directorate S is in charge of Customer relations. The Translation Directorates also subsume functions responsible for Quality Management, Language Applications and Interinstitutional cooperation. Directorate R (Resources) covers new technologies, internal administrative matters, budget and finance, informatics and professional and organizational development while Directorate S manages customer relations, workflow systems, demand management, external translation, editing, evaluation and analysis, and web rationalization task force. In particular, there is a need to balance demand management, budgetary resources, internal and external translation flows, as well as interinstitutional cooperation.

[19] As at 1.06.2017 https://ec.europa.eu/info/sites/info/files/organisation_chart_translation_june_2017_en.pdf (Accessed 2017-07-01).

The very existence of these functions points to their recognition as important (see also Prieto Ramos 2017 [this volume] on translation service managers).

At a more local level, workflow management ensures quality control at the pre-translation, translation and post-translation stage. At the pre-translation stage, quality assurance mechanisms may involve planning, source file preparation (technically and linguistically through editing), terminology resources, translation resources, and project management resources (Drugan 2013: 77–79); in particular, the assignment of a job to a suitable translator (Prieto Ramos 2015: 23). At the translation stage in the institutional context, it may mean sufficient support for translators with terminology assistance, research by assistants, consultations with national experts, etc., as well as deadline management.[20] Workflow management also covers quality control and assessment, especially at the post-translation stage, including (bilingual) revision, (monolingual) review, random checks by quality officers, legal linguistic revision by lawyer-linguists, editing of source texts by native speakers to improve their quality,[21] as well as strategic planning in relation to quality control, e.g. the introduction and monitoring of performance indicators, such as a customer satisfaction rate, deadline compliance rate or correction rate (cf. DGT 2016b).

3.2.3 Quality of people: translators and support staff

The key components of quality include the human resources involved in the provision of translation services.[22] Such human resources cover translators, revisers, as well as supporting roles, including linguistic assistants,[23] terminologists (see Stefaniak 2017 [this volume]), quality officers/controllers (see Drugan et al. 2018), and national experts.

Translators can be divided into staff (in-house) translators and external translators (contractors). In-house translators are employed with the dual roles of translators and revisers. In-house translation services are available in the majority of EU institutions, e.g. in the European Commission, the Council, the European Parliament, the Court of Justice, the Economic and Social Committee, the Court of Auditors; while other bodies are services by the Luxembourg-based

[20] See the DGT's recent commitment to ensure shorter deadlines for "political priority documents" and to increase the deadline compliance rate (% of pages produced within the deadline) from 95% in 2009 to 99% (DGT 2016b: 6, 9).

[21] For example, the European Commission plans to increase the editing of its major initiatives from 12% in 2015 to 65% in 2020 (DGT 2016b).

[22] See Svoboda (2008) on the human factor in the European Commission's DGT.

[23] See e.g. a notice of competition http://eur-lex.europa.eu/legal-content/EN/TXT/HTML/?uri=OJ:C:2016:151A:FULL&from=EN (Accessed 2017-07-01).

Translation Centre for the Bodies of the European Union. EU institutions have a long tradition of recruiting, training and managing translators. In-house translators were already employed in the High Authority of the European Coal and Steel Community established by the Treaty of Paris in 1952 and over the decades they substantially grew in numbers and raised their status, becoming permanent officials in the late 1950s (European Commission 2010: 18).[24] In light of the highly specialized nature of texts, the role of translators' specializations have been growing in importance since the 1990s (European Commission 2010: 12, 13). In-house translators are employed by most institutions after they pass the EPSO[25] competition and meet the requirements specified in the competition notice. In general, candidates have to meet the following requirements: a bachelor's degree and a perfect command of their mother tongue (C2 level) and two official EU languages (C1 level), of which at least one should be a procedural language.[26] Interestingly, no professional experience is officially required;[27] however, the translator's profile at the European Commission's website explicitly mentions thematic skills required to deal with political, economic, financial, legal, scientific and technical texts.[28] The procedure comprises three stages: (1) computer-based multiple-choice question tests on verbal, numerical and abstract reasoning tests in language 1 (L1) and comprehension L2 and L3; (2) two translation tests into L1 – which are usually general but very idiomatic in nature and (3) three tests in L2 in the assessment centre (oral presentation, competency-based interview and group exercise) to test general competencies, such as analysis and problem solving, communicating, delivering quality and results, learning and development, prioritizing and organizing, resilience, working with others, and leadership.[29] At a first glance, the requirements may not seem excessively strict (e.g. no previous translation experience required and a general text to translate); however, due to financially attractive job prospects, the competition is tough in most countries and good candidates tend to be preselected. In-house translators are subject to continuous professional training to deepen their subject matter exper-

[24] PROTOCOL (NO 7) ON THE PRIVILEGES AND IMMUNITIES OF THE EUROPEAN UNION TO THE TREATY OF ROME, 1957.

[25] https://epso.europa.eu/.

[26] https://ec.europa.eu/info/jobs-european-commission/translator-profile_en (Accessed 2017-07-01).

[27] NB: notices of competitions explicitly state "No professional experience required", e.g. http://eur-lex.europa.eu/legal-content/EN/TXT/HTML/?uri=OJ:C:2016:205A:FULL&from=EN (Accessed 2017-07-01).

[28] https://ec.europa.eu/info/jobs-european-commission/translator-profile_en (Accessed 2017-07-01).

[29] See e.g. Notice of open competitions: http://eur-lex.europa.eu/legal-content/EN/TXT/HTML/?uri=OJ:C:2016:205A:FULL&from=EN (Accessed 2017-07-01).

tise and acquire new language skills, including joint interinstitutional training events (DGT 2016b: 8, 15). In line with the European Commission's commitment, DGT planned to reduce its staffing levels by the end of 2016 by 10% compared to 2012 (DGT 2016a: 14).

The requirements are higher in the Court of Justice of the European Union, which employs only LAWYER-LINGUISTS as in-house and external translators (see Koźbiał 2017 [this volume]). Lawyer-linguists are required to have a law degree and a good command of three official languages (however, no formal education in languages is required) and, like translators, they have to go through the EPSO competition. It is worth noting that while the Commission does not require its translators to have a legal background to translate EU legislation, it employs lawyer-linguists to check translations. On the other hand, the Court does – it employs lawyer-linguists to translate judgments and other court documents. Lawyer-linguists' tasks differ across institutions and their role could be best defined in much broader terms as legal-linguistic revision. The term *lawyer-linguist* is now used across all institutions; however, they used to have distinct names: *legal revisers* in the European Commission, *jurist-linguists* in the Council of the European Union and *reviser lawyer-linguists* in the European Parliament (Šarčević & Robertson 2013: 186, 188, 189). Legal-linguistic revision has a broader scope than the typical bilingual revision and may include a revision of the source text, linguistic and legal consistency check of a target text with other language versions as well as an occasional check of all language versions for consistency (Šarčević & Robertson 2013: 186).[30] Lawyer-linguists are also involved in the early interventions of drafts at the pre-translation stage to facilitate their translation into all the official languages (Šarčević & Robertson 2013: 187).

First SUPPORT STAFF included typists, stenographers and revisers in the 1950s while the role of the terminologist emerged in the Commission in the 1960s (European Commission 2010: 12, 21). Terminologists are involved in ad-hoc terminology work to support translators on the job, usually more difficult specialized terms, as well as in systematic terminology work, which consists of creating term records in term bases (see Stefaniak 2017 [this volume]). Linguistic assistants assist translators and lawyer-linguists in translation and revision by pre-processing or post-processing texts in IT tools, databases and templates, acting as IT helpdesk/coordinator, managing linguistic and legal-linguistic information and documentation (reference documents, maintaining resources, updating

[30] See also an example of a notice of open competitions for lawyer-linguists http://eur-lex.europa.eu/legal-content/EN/TXT/HTML/?uri=OJ:C:2016:457A:FULL&from=EN (Accessed 2017-07-01).

translation memories, compiling information, and corresponding with national experts), and incorporating changes in legislation.[31]

External translators are selected through open calls for tenders[32] and include both freelancers and translation agencies. The discussion below is illustrated with the Commission's procedures. Award criteria are based on the "most economically advantageous tender".[33] Tenderers have to evidence that they and/or their translators, revisers and reviewers have: (1) the required level of tertiary education – usually, a Bachelor's degree in any area; and (2) proven translation experience in the domain required in the specific language combination, e.g. 3,000 pages over the period of 3 years.[34] Contractors sign 1-year framework contracts which may be renewed for further three 1-year contracts (a total of 4 years). Contractors are offered orders in the order as they appear in the ranking which is re-ranked on a monthly basis according to the average quality of translations in the previous month, based on in-house evaluation (the so-called dynamic assessment system).[35] External translations are usually reviewed, in most cases some parts of it only, e.g. the EC's DGT revises only 10% of the document, from 2 to 10 pages (DGT 2012: 17), even though it used to revise entire texts until recently (Strandvik 2017b). The dynamic ranking of external contractors should be viewed positively as a step forward in controlling and assuring the quality of external translations. After the award of tender, some initial period of unstable and unpredictable quality may be expected which should level out after a few re-rankings, allowing institutions to identify underperforming contractors, who naturally fall down in the ranking. For example, after the award of the Omnibus tender in 2016, the Commission's DGT experienced a fall of "very good" and "good" marks on external translations from the very high level of 94%[36] in 2015 to 87% in 2016 as well as non-compliance with deadlines, the problems which were addressed through remedial measures, such as penalties and contract termination.[37]

---

[31] Cf. http://eur-lex.europa.eu/legal-content/EN/TXT/HTML/?uri=OJ:C:2016:151A:FULL&from=EN (Accessed 2017-07-01).

[32] It is worth noting that EU tender procedures and specifications in respect of translations are regarded as good practices in some national contexts due to the significant role of quality criteria in addition to price (cf. Wołoszyk 2017).

[33] Cf. Omnibus, op. cit., p. 16.

[34] Cf. Omnibus, op. cit., p. 21.

[35] Cf. https://cdt.europa.eu/en/dynamic-ranking (Accessed 2017-07-01).

[36] It is worth noting that before 2016 the freelance quality was consistently growing from 91% in 2011 to 94% in 2015; cf. DGT's *Annual Activity Report 2015*. Ref. Ares(2016)1818629 – 18/04/2016, p. 8.

[37] DGT, European Commission. *Annual Activity Report 2016*. Ref. Ares(2017)1826615 - 05/04/2017, pp. 4–5, 9.

On the positive side, it should be highlighted that the criterion of quality has gained in importance over the years. First, by raising the quality level required of external translators through the replacement of the "Acceptable" mark (6/10) with the "Below standard" descriptor and the "Below standard" (4/10) with "Insufficient".[38] Secondly, the mechanism has evolved to give more weight to quality over price – currently 70/30[39] (e.g. a change from the first 50/50 and next 60/40). Yet the excessively high price competition on some markets, especially from newcomers, has reduced the prices to the level which has driven some more experienced contractors away.

To illustrate this claim, we can analyze the price ranges in contracts for the translation of EU texts relating to the policies and administration of the European Union (OMNIBUS-15)[40] awarded in 2016 by the European Commission. What is most striking is the high variation of prices between the new accession countries and most of the EU-15 countries which have more mature freelance markets. For example, the highest prices apply to Gaelic (due to the shortage of translators) and Northern European languages – Swedish, Danish, Finnish, Dutch, e.g. EN-GA (26.45–60.23 EUR per page[41]), EN-SV (€33.5–58), EN-DA (€32.45–56.63), with top prices reaching 60 EUR per page, while the lowest prices are offered by contractors from Romania, Bulgaria, Latvia, Croatia, Poland, Hungary, Czech Republic, e.g. FR-RO (€6–14.99), EN-RO (€8–24), RO-EN (€9–11.99), BG-EN (€10–12,99), HR-EN (€13–16.5 EUR), FR-PL (€12–13); DE-PL (€12–15), with the lowest price reaching 6 EUR, that is 10 times less than the top price.[42] What is also notable is the low variation of prices for some language pairs, e.g. DA-EN (€33.9–37.8), FI-EN (€31.5–33.9), DE-DA (€44.75–46.75) and high variation for some other, e.g. EN-EL (€12.5–40), EN-MT (€11.5–48.5). It should be noted that even the highest external prices (the range of €50–60) are much cheaper than in-house prices, estimated in the Court of Auditors' Special Report 2006 at €119 per page at the Parliament, €194 at the Commission and €276 at the Council in 2005.

The current and future policy of EU institutions is to significantly increase the involvement of external translators through outsourcing in order to reduce costs or, in some cases, to meet peak demand. Outsourcing practices differ across institutions; yet there is a discernible upward trend within the EU combined with in-

[38] European Commission, 06.2016, *Instructions for Users*, pp. 41–42.

[39] Omnibus, op. cit., p. 22.

[40] Contract notice 2015/S 037-062226, http://ted.europa.eu/udl?uri=TED:NOTICE:62226-2015:TEXT:EN:HTML (Accessed 2017-07-01).

[41] 1,500 characters of the source text, excluding spaces (Omnibus, op. cit.).

[42] https://ec.europa.eu/info/sites/info/files/omnibus_15_2015.pdf (Accessed 2017-07-01).

house staff reductions. The outsourcing practice is not new and has been put into place to cope with an insufficient internal capacity to meet translation requests. The rate of outsourcing was 22% for the Commission, 33% for the Parliament and 0% for the Council for all languages in 2003; the rate of outsourcing in 2005 fell to 20% for the Commission, increased to 36% for the Parliament and amounted to 2% for the Council (Court of Auditors 2006). The outsourcing trends were much higher for new languages (the 2004 enlargement) than for the EU-15 due to delays in the recruitment process. As early as in 2003–2004, the outsourcing objective was set by the Commission and the Parliament to reach 40% and 30%, respectively (Court of Auditors 2006), but was suspended in 2004 by the Commission due to a fall in demand. The outsourcing trend is planned to increase in the coming years. For example, according to the European Commission DGT's Strategic Plan 2016–2020, the outsourcing rate of the DGT is targeted to increase progressively from 27% in 2015 to 37% of total pages translated by DGT in 2020 (DGT 2016b: 11).

The upward outsourcing trend is associated with quality risk. In-house translation is much more expensive but is characterized, as argued by the Court of Auditors in 2006, by higher quality: "the quality of internal translation is recognized to be higher" (Court of Auditors 2006). In-house translators can ensure a better contextualization of translations and enjoy the benefit of dedicated trainings, internal resources and better integration of such resources, as well as having insider knowledge. Secondly, it is also a well-known fact among freelancers that some agencies win tenders with experienced (and expensive) translators' CVs but outsource actual work to cheaper and less experienced translators,[43] even though some measures to curb this phenomenon have been put in place recently. Thirdly, while most institutions claim that they outsource "non-priority" texts, e.g. see the European Parliament "Documents of the highest priority, i.e. legislative documents and documents to be put to the vote in plenary are, as far as internal resources permit, translated in-house. Other types of documents, especially administrative texts, are frequently outsourced."[44], it is not always the case (see Strandvik 2017b, on a move towards outsourcing policy documents and legislation) and the situation varies from one language unit to another, depending on internal capacity.

[43]See for example discussions on Proz.com: http://www.proz.com/forum/business_issues/291854-agencies_that_ask_for_too_much_info.html#2472785 (Accessed 2017-07-01).

[44]http://www.europarl.europa.eu/pdf/multilinguisme/EP_translators_en.pdf (Accessed 2017-07-01).

3.2.4 Quality of resources (tools)

In order to ensure consistency and the standardization of translations, EU institutions invest considerable funds in the development of technological, terminological and linguistic resources which support translators during the translation process. Such resources enable EU institutions to regulate and control the language and format of STs and TTs. They ensure terminological consistency, uniform institutional style and textual patterns in translation with a view to keeping variation and idiosyncrasy to the minimum (e.g. Biel 2014: 70). Tools differ to some extent between institutions and include among others:

- terminological resources: IATE,[45] EuroVoc;[46]
- databases of documents: EUR-Lex,[47] Curia;[48]
- style guides: joint for all the institutions, e.g. *Interinstitutional Style Guide*,[49] institution-specific and language-specific style guides (e.g. *Vademecum tłumacza*[50] for Polish; see also Svoboda 2017a, Svoboda 2017b [this volume]);
- CAT tools (SDL Trados Studio), translation memories[51] and translation memory management system (EURAMIS);[52]
- machine translation system MT@EC;
- workflow and document management tools: *Poetry, ManDesk, Tradesk, DGT Vista* (European Commission 2016).

One of the most important components is the interface which integrates resources in one place to ensure a good speed of information retrieval. I will discuss selected resources below (for more detailed information see European Commission 2016).

[45] http://iate.europa.eu
[46] http://eurovoc.europa.eu
[47] http://eur-lex.europa.eu
[48] https://curia.europa.eu/jcms/jcms/j_6/pl
[49] http://publications.europa.eu/code/en/en-000100.htm
[50] http://ec.europa.eu/translation/polish/guidelines/documents/styleguide_polish_dgt_pl.pdf
[51] DGT publishes parts of its translation memories in 24 languages: https://ec.europa.eu/jrc/en/language-technologies/dgt-translation-memory#StatisticsfortheDGTTranslationMemory (Accessed 2017-07-01).
[52] Euramis, managed by the European Commission, is a system storing translation memories of most EU institutions; it searches and retrieves segments with matches; http://ec.europa.eu/dpo-register/details.htm?id=41727 (Accessed 2017-07-01).

As for the **CAT** tools, most EU institutions use SDL Trados Studio 2015, which was customized to the specific needs of EU translators (Trousil 2017). A new server-based CAT environment is planned to be introduced in 2018–2019 (DGT 2016b: 7). The CAT tool is integrated with IATE through the term recognition window (Trousil 2017).

IATE (Inter-Active Terminology for Europe) is a major terminological achievement of EU institutions, which began to be built in 2000, used internally from 2004 and made public in 2007. It is a termbase of about 1.4 million multilingual entries, integrating the terminological resources of key EU institutions, including Eurodicautom, TIS, Euterpe, Euroterms, and CDCTERM.[53] It is a "one-stop consultation" resource for the institutions, with two interfaces: public and internal (Trousil 2017). One of its key functionalities is the evaluation of terminological information with reliability ratings and labels, such as "preferred", "admitted", "deprecated", "obsolete", as well as references with sources of information. The institutions are working on new improved IATE 2 to be released in 2018[54] but it should be stressed that the quality and functionality of IATE have improved significantly over the years. Other multilingual terminological resources include **EuroVoc**, a multilingual multi-disciplinary thesaurus on the activities of the European Union, with a first edition in 1984.[55] It is also worth noting that some resources, e.g. electronic dictionaries and specialized databases, are developed by external contractors selected through tender procedures.[56]

Another type of resource, **Tradesk** (Translator's Desktop), is a database with a document handling tool and a collection of translation comments entered by translators, facilitates communication between the coordinating translator and translators from the same or other institutions working on the same translation and its purpose is defined as "[i]mprove communication and exchange of best practices between translators of different institutions working on inter-institutional legislative proposals, in order to avoid double work and improve consistency and quality of EU legislation".[57] The Tradesk interface provides in-house translators with access to reference documents, allows for comparisons between different versions and for the annotation of translation with information from experts and clarifications from the requester (Trousil 2017). Access to documents is also available through such tools as the document search engine DGT Vista, the

[53] http://iate.europa.eu/about_IATE.html (Accessed 2017-07-01).

[54] http://iate.europa.eu/IATE_2.html (Accessed 2017-07-01).

[55] http://eurovoc.europa.eu/drupal/?q=abouteurovoc&cl=en (Accessed 2017-07-01).

[56] Cf. http://ted.europa.eu/udl?uri=TED:NOTICE:398481-2016:TEXT:EN:HTML (Accessed 2017-07-01).

[57] http://ec.europa.eu/dpo-register/details.htm?id=35572 (Accessed 2017-07-01).

text search tool DocFinder, the terminological metasearch tool Quest Metasearch (Trousil 2017), as well as through more specialized publicly accessible databases, e.g. the legislation repository EUR-Lex.

MT@EC is an online statistical machine translation system based on Moses and released in 2013 (Mai 2016), which translates from and into EU official languages and is made available for free to public administration and universities of the European Masters' in Translation network in EU countries;[58] however, interestingly, it is not available to external contractors. One of the DGT's strategic objectives is to increase the use of its system by doubling direct requests for MT@EC by individual users and web services to 4 million pages in 2020 (DGT 2016b: 9). The MT@EC system was trained on EU corpora (i.e. Euramis with 1 billion segments (Mai 2016)) and gives relatively good results on EU-related texts, except for highly inflected languages. The involvement of machine translation differs from one institution to another. For example, the German Language Department of the DGT uses it selectively in press releases, reports, and general communications but not for legislation and other legal texts (Mai 2016). It is mainly applied as "lexical inspiration" and a tool to speed up work by reducing typing and searches; however, its disadvantages include attention focusing on different (mainly linguistic) types of errors (Mai 2016). Some translators also note that the use of machine translation output and a shift from translation to post-editing prevent the deep processing of and submergence in the source/target texts which are typical of human translation (cf. O'Brien et al. 2014). It is worth noting that MT@EC is a predecessor to **eTranslation**, part of the Connecting Europe Facility, which will incorporate neural machine translation solutions and will pool much larger resources.

To sum up, the volume and quality of technological, linguistic and terminological resources are growing and they help translators ensure the consistency and standardization of translations and increase the efficiency of their work. Yet it should be stressed that some of the tools are not available at all or in full to external translators, which may adversely affect the quality of outsourced translations.

[58] https://ec.europa.eu/info/resources-partners/machine-translation-public-administrations-mtec_en (Accessed 2017-07-01).

4 Concluding remarks: reframing of quality and threat to quality

Over the last decade EU institutions have boosted the profile of quality, which is evidenced in an increasing number of policies and guidelines addressing the quality of EU translation, as well as in attempts to quantify quality through performance indicators, such as correction rates and customer satisfaction rates. One of the promising developments is the reframing of quality discourse by the explicit linking of translation quality at the textual level to genres and genre clusters, with a resulting shift of focus from equivalence to clarity and textual fit. On the other hand, such classifications may be seen as triggered by the need to prioritize documents, as part of the fit-for-purpose approach, in order to prudently manage resources and costs in line with the required level of quality. Cost effective measures towards translation products are coupled with measures at the service provision level of translation quality, including selective translation policies and demand management, the growing burden on in-house staff, staffing reductions combined with the increasing rate of outsourcing, as well as the growing use of machine translation and its unknown impact on quality. This may pose a threat to quality in the long run.

Acknowledgement

This work was supported by the National Science Centre (NCN) under Grant 2014/14/E/HS2/00782.

References

Biel, Łucja. 2011a. Jakość przekładu prawnego i prawniczego w świetle normy europejskiej PN-EN 15038 oraz hipotezy uniwersaliów translatorycznych [Quality of legal translation through the lens of EN 15038 standard and the hypotheses of translation universals]. *Rocznik Przekładoznawczy* 6. 13–28.

Biel, Łucja. 2011b. Training translators or translation service providers? EN 15038:2006 standard of translation services and its training implications. *The Journal of Specialised Translation* 16. 61–76.

Biel, Łucja. 2014. *Lost in the Eurofog: the textual fit of translated law.* Frankfurt am Main: Peter Lang.

Biel, Łucja. 2017. Genre analysis and translation. In Kirsten Malmkjær (ed.), *The Routledge handbook of translation studies and linguistics.* London: Routledge.

Bobek, Michal. 2009. Corrigenda in the Official Journal of the European Union: Community law as quicksand. *European Law Review* 34. 950–962.

Chesterman, Andrew. 2004. Hypotheses about translation universals. In Gyde Hansen, Kirsten Malmkjær & Daniel Gile (eds.), *Claims, changes and challenges in Translation Studies. Selected contributions from the EST Congress, Copenhagen 2001*, 1–13. Amsterdam: John Benjamins.

Colina, Sonia. 2009. Further evidence for a functionalist approach to translation quality evaluation. *Target* 21(2). 235–264. DOI:10.1075/target.21.2.02col

Craith, Máiréad Nic. 2006. *Europe and the politics of language. citizens, migrants and outsiders.* Basingstoke: Palgrave McMillian.

Directorate-General for Translation (DGT), European Commission. 2008. *Guide for external translators.* http://ec.europa.eu/translation/documents/guide_contractors_en.pdf, accessed 2012-5-28.

Directorate-General for Translation (DGT), European Commission. 2012. *Quantifying quality costs and the cost of poor quality in translation. quality efforts and the consequences of poor quality in the European Commission's Directorate-General for Translation.* Luxembourg: Publications Office of the European Union.

Directorate-General for Translation (DGT), European Commission. 2015. *DGT translation quality guidelines. DGT.IS/IP/DH/GH/th-(2015)5977178.* http://ec.europa.eu/translation/maltese/guidelines/documents/dgt_translation_quality_guidelines_en.pdf, accessed 2017-7-1.

Directorate-General for Translation (DGT), European Commission. 2016a. *Management plan 2016. DGT. Ref. Ares(2016)2103398 - 03/05/201.* https://ec.europa.eu/info/sites/info/files/management-plan-2016-dg-dgt-may2016_en.pdf, accessed 2017-7-1.

Directorate-General for Translation (DGT), European Commission. 2016b. *Strategic plan 2016-2020. DG Translation. Ref. Ares(2016)1329034 - 16/03/201.* https://ec.europa.eu/info/sites/info/files/strategic-plan-2016-2020-dg-t_march2016_en.pdf, accessed 2017-7-1.

Doczekalska, Agnieszka. 2009. Drafting and interpretation of EU law: paradoxes of legal multilingualism. In Günther Grewendorf & Monika Rathert (eds.), *Formal linguistics and law*, 339–370. Berlin: de Gruyter.

Dollerup, Cay. 2001. Complexities of EU language work. *Perspectives: Studies in Translatology* 9(4). 271–292.

Drugan, Joanna. 2013. *Quality in professional translation: assessment and improvement.* London: Bloomsbury.

Drugan, Joanna, Ingemar Strandvik & Erkka Vuorinen. 2018. Translation quality, quality management and agency: principles and practice in the European Union institutions. In Joss Moorkens, Sheila Castilho, Stephen Doherty & Federico Gaspari (eds.), *Translation quality assessment: from principles to practice.* Berlin: Springer.

European Commission. 1997. *Legislative drafting. A Commission manual.* http://ec.europa.eu/smart-regulation/better_regulation/documents/legis_draft_comm_en.pdf, accessed 2017-7-1.

European Commission. 2010. *Translation at the European Commission — A history.* Luxembourg: Office for Official Publications of the European Communities.

European Court of Auditors. 2006. Special Report No 9/2006 concerning translation expenditure incurred by the Commission, the Parliament and the Council. *Official Journal of the European Union* (C 284).

Felici, Annarita. 2010. Translating EU law: legal issues and multiple dynamics. *Perspectives: Studies in Translatology* 18(2). 95–108. DOI:http://dx.doi.org/10.1080/09076761003668289

General Secretariat of the Council (GSC). 2012. *The language service of the General Secretariat of the Council of the European Union.* Brussels: Consilium. DOI:10.2860/79193

Hanzl, Jan & John Beaven. 2017. Quality assurance at the Council of the EU's Translation Service. In Tomáš Svoboda, Łucja Biel & Krzysztof Łoboda (eds.), *Quality aspects in institutional translation* (Translation and Multilingual Natural Language Processing 8), 139–153. Berlin: Language Science Press. DOI:10.5281/zenodo.1048196

Hermans, Theo. 2007. *The conference of the tongues.* Manchester: St. Jerome.

House, Juliane. 2015. *Translation quality assessment. Past and present.* London & New York: Routledge.

ISO 17100:2015. 2015. *Translation services – Requirements for translation services.* Geneva: ISO. http://www.iso.org/iso/catalogue_detail.htm?csnumber=59149.

Jiménez-Crespo, Miguel A. 2017. How much would you like to pay? reframing and expanding the notion of translation quality through crowdsourcing and volunteer approaches. *Perspectives. Studies in Translation Theory and Practice* 25(3). 478–491. DOI:10.1080/0907676X.2017.1285948

Kang, Ji-Hae. 2011. Institutional translation. In Mona Baker & Gabriela Saldanha (eds.), *Routledge encyclopedia of Translation Studies*, 141–145. New York: Routledge.

Kapko, Mirosława. 2005. Konsekwencje błędów w tłumaczeniu aktów prawa wspólnotowego na język polski [Consequences of errors in translations of Community law into Polish]. *Prawo i Podatki Unii Europejskiej* 11. 2–8.

Koskinen, Kaisa. 2000. Institutional illusions. translating in the EU Commission. *The Translator* 6(1). 49–65.

Koskinen, Kaisa. 2008. *Translating institutions. an ethnographic study of EU translation.* Manchester: St. Jerome.

Kotler, Philip & Kevin Lane Keller. 2006. *Marketing management.* 12th edn. New Jersey: Pearson.

Koźbiał, Dariusz. 2017. Two-tiered approach to quality assurance in legal translation at the Court of Justice of the European Union. In Tomáš Svoboda, Łucja Biel & Krzysztof Łoboda (eds.), *Quality aspects in institutional translation* (Translation and Multilingual Natural Language Processing 8), 155–174. Berlin: Language Science Press. DOI:10.5281/zenodo.1048198

Krzyżanowski, Michał & Ruth Wodak. 2011. Political strategies and language policies: the European Union Lisbon Strategy and its implications for the EU's language and multilingualism policy. *Language Policy* 10. 115–136. DOI:10.1007s/10993-011-9196-5

Mai, Katja. 2016. *Use of MT/@EC by translators in the European Commission. 2nd ELRC Conference, Brussels, 26.10.2016.* http://www.lr-coordination.eu/sites/default/files/Brussels_conference/Mai-K_ELRC-MT(at)EC%20in%20DGT_26_10_2016_K.%20Mai.pdf, accessed 2017-7-1.

Martin, Tim. 2007. Managing risks and resources: a down-to-earth view of revision. *The Journal of Specialised Translation* 8. 57–63.

Mason, Ian. 2004 [2003]. Text parameters in translation: transitivity and institutional cultures. In Lawrence Venuti (ed.), *The Translation Studies reader*, 2nd edn., 470–481. New York/London: Routledge.

Mattila, Heikki E. S. 2013. *Comparative legal linguistics. Language of law, Latin and modern lingua francas.* 2nd edn. London: Routledge.

O'Brien, Sharon, Laura Winther Balling, Michael Carl, Michel Simard & Lucia Specia (eds.). 2014. *Post-editing of machine translation: processes and applications.* Newcastle upon Tyne: Cambridge Scholars Publishing.

Pozzo, Barbara. 2012. The impact of multilingualism on the harmonization of European public law. *European Review of Private Law* 20(5/6). 1181–1183.

Prieto Ramos, Fernando. 2015. Quality assurance in legal translation: evaluating process, competence and product in the pursuit of adequacy. *International Journal for the Semiotics of Law* 28. 11–30.

Prieto Ramos, Fernando. 2017. The evolving role of institutional translation service managers in quality assurance: Profiles and challenges. In Tomáš Svoboda, Łucja Biel & Krzysztof Łoboda (eds.), *Quality aspects in institutional translation* (Translation and Multilingual Natural Language Processing 8), 59–74. Berlin: Language Science Press. DOI:10.5281/zenodo.1048188

Robertson, Colin. 2015. Eu multilingual law: interfaces of law, language and culture. In Susan Šarčević (ed.), *Language and culture in EU law. Multidisciplinary perspectives*, 33–51. Farnham: Ashgate.

Šarčević, Susan. 1997. *New approach to legal translation*. The Hague: Kluwer Law International.

Šarčević, Susan. 2007. Making multilingualism work in the enlarged Europe Union. In Krzysztof Kredens & Stanisław Goźdź-Roszkowski (eds.), *Language and the law: International outlooks*, 35–54. Frankfurt am Main: Peter Lang.

Šarčević, Susan & Colin Robertson. 2013. The work of lawyer-linguists in the EU Institutions. In Anabel Borja Albi & Fernando Prieto Ramos (eds.), *Legal translation in context: Professional issues and prospects*, 181–202.

for Standardization (CEN), European Committee. 2006. *EN 15038:2006 Translation services – service requirements*. Brussels: CEN.

Stefaniak, Karolina. 2013. Multilingual legal drafting, translators' choices and the principle of lesser evil. *Meta. The Translators' Journal* 58(1). 58–65.

Stefaniak, Karolina. 2017. Terminology work in the European Commission: Ensuring high-quality translation in a multilingual environment. In Tomáš Svoboda, Łucja Biel & Krzysztof Łoboda (eds.), *Quality aspects in institutional translation* (Translation and Multilingual Natural Language Processing 8), 109–121. Berlin: Language Science Press. DOI:10.5281/zenodo.1048192

Strandvik, Ingemar. 2015. On quality in EU multilingual lawmaking. In Susan Šarčević (ed.), *Language and culture in EU Law. Multidisciplinary perspectives*, 141–165. Farnham: Ashgate.

Strandvik, Ingemar. 2017a. Evaluation of outsourced translations. State of play in the European Commission's Directorate-General for Translation (DGT). In Tomáš Svoboda, Łucja Biel & Krzysztof Łoboda (eds.), *Quality aspects in institutional translation* (Translation and Multilingual Natural Language Processing 8), 123–137. Berlin: Language Science Press. DOI:10.5281/zenodo.1048194

Strandvik, Ingemar. 2017b. Towards a more structured approach to quality assurance: DGT's quality journey. In Fernando Prieto Ramos (ed.), *Institutional translation for international governance: enhancing quality in multilingual legal communication*, 51–62. London: Bloomsbury.

Svoboda, Tomáš. 2008. Ubi sunt homines? Poznámky k řízení kvality překladů u Generálního ředitelství pro překlad Evropské komise [Ubi sunt homines? On Translation Quality Management at the European Commission's Directorate-General for Translation]. In Alena Ďuricová (ed.), *Od textu k prekladu II*, 143–151. Prague: Jednota tlumočníků a překladatelů.

Svoboda, Tomáš. 2017a. Translation manuals and style guides as quality assurance indicators: The case of the European Commission's Directorate-General for Translation. In Tomáš Svoboda, Łucja Biel & Krzysztof Łoboda (eds.), *Quality aspects in institutional translation* (Translation and Multilingual Natural Language Processing 8), 75–107. Berlin: Language Science Press. DOI:10.5281/zenodo.1048190

Svoboda, Tomáš. 2017b. Translation manuals and style guides as quality assurance indicators:The case of the European Commission's Directorate-General for Translation. In Tomáš Svoboda, Łucja Biel & Krzysztof Łoboda (eds.), *Quality aspects in institutional translation* (Translation and Multilingual Natural Language Processing 8), 75–107. Berlin: Language Science Press. DOI:10.5281/zenodo.1048190

Tosi, Arturo. 2002. The europeanization of the Italian language by the European Union. In Anna Laura Lepschy & Arturo Tosi (eds.), *Multilingualism in Italy, past and present*, 170–194. Oxford: Legenda.

Trosborg, Anna. 1997. Translating hybrid political texts. In Anna Trosborg (ed.), *Text typology and translation*, 145–158. Amsterdam: John Benjamins.

Trousil, Štěpán. 2017. *Dealing with terminology in DGT with special focus on IATE.* Spain. Paper read at 7th Seminario de Traducción Jurídica Para Organizaciones Internacionales. 22.3.2017.

van Els, Theodorus Johannes Maria. 2001. The European Union, its institutions and its languages: some language political observations. *Current Issues in Language Planning* 2(4). 311–360.

Vandepitte, Sonia. 2017. Translation product quality: A conceptual analysis. In Tomáš Svoboda, Łucja Biel & Krzysztof Łoboda (eds.), *Quality aspects in institutional translation* (Translation and Multilingual Natural Language Processing 8), 15–29. Berlin: Language Science Press. DOI:10.5281/zenodo.1048180

Wagner, Emma, Svend Bech & Jesús M. Martínez. 2002. *Translating for the European Union institutions. Translation practices explained.* Manchester: St. Jerome.

Wołoszyk, Wojciech. 2017. Kryteria jakościowe oraz podział zamówienia na części w przetargach publicznych na usługi tłumaczeń pisemnych [quality criteria and a division of a contract into parts in public tenders for translation services]. *Zamawiający* (July-August). 41–45.

Chapter 4

The evolving role of institutional translation service managers in quality assurance: Profiles and challenges

Fernando Prieto Ramos
University of Geneva

The diversification of translation services, tools and quality expectations in an increasingly globalized translation industry has accentuated the significance of translation quality assurance (TQA) processes and their management. This paper focuses on the profile of institutional translation service managers from a holistic TQA perspective. After a short account of their most common duties as described in sample vacancy notices from various international organizations, including senior service managers and mid-level language unit heads, the role of the latter as competence and process managers responsible for translation quality in specific languages is analyzed in more detail. The data compiled in 24 interviews with mid-level managers serve to outline an inventory of their main TQA-related functions and challenges, and lead to conclusions on their growing relevance and expected expertise in this evolving field.

1 Introduction: managing translation quality in a changing landscape

Translation management functions have been the subject of little research in Translation Studies. Yet, they play a key role in monitoring translation quality assurance (TQA) processes in a context of increasing diversification of translation services and greater automatization of production workflows. The growing differentiation of translation quality and pricing levels according to market segment and client needs has further reinforced the significance of translation

Fernando Prieto Ramos. 2017. The evolving role of institutional translation service managers in quality assurance: Profiles and challenges. In Tomáš Svoboda, Łucja Biel & Krzysztof Łoboda (eds.), *Quality aspects in institutional translation*, 59–74. Berlin: Language Science Press. DOI:10.5281/zenodo.1048188

management. These trends have been shaped by a number of interrelated factors, in particular, heightened global interconnectivity, an exponential surge in information flows and multilingual content needs in multiple formats, and the development of technological tools, including online translation applications and crowdsourcing platforms (see e.g. García 2015 and Jiménez-Crespo 2017). Görög (2014: 388) summarizes the industry perspective in the following terms: "The only way to offer large amounts of information and goods in multiple languages fast while staying within reasonable budgets is by making a compromise and provide content with different levels of quality using new translation channels and translation technology."

For translation service providers (TSPs) in the private sector, which has been at the frontline of this diversification, providing less-than-maximal quality is not a taboo but may prove a fit solution depending on job specifications and market conditions (see e.g. Wright 2006; Gouadec 2010; O'Brien 2012; Drugan 2013; Fields et al. 2014). It is not surprising that the last few years have witnessed the emergence of translation quality standards specifically aimed at certifying TSPs in this more diversified and globalized market: the European EN 15038:2006 (for Standardization (CEN) 2006) and its successor, the international ISO 17100:2015. These standards do not provide any variables to define or measure quality, but focus on two key elements that contribute to ensuring quality translation: workflow specifications (including systematic revision), and definition of roles and competence requirements for the different actors involved in the service provision process.

These industry developments (and their conceptual underpinnings) are finding their way into translator training programmes and are gradually permeating the translation services of public institutions, especially in situations where budgetary constraints push them towards cost-benefit considerations typically found in the private sector. The translation services of international organizations are no exception. In light of increasing productivity demands and strain on resources, traditional models based on ideals of absolute quality are nuanced by efficiency considerations of content prioritization and quality control modulation according to potential risk or impact of translations (on risk management in translation projects, see e.g. Dunne 2013; Canfora & Ottmann 2015). Although this approach is not new, it is becoming more explicit and widespread, as illustrated by Prioux & Rochard (2007) in their "economy of revision" at the Organization for Economic Cooperation and Development. The translation services of the European Union (EU) institutions provide the most clear example of this trend: the addition of nine official languages in 2004 and three more in 2007 compounded the need to streamline practices and triggered "a move towards a more conscious, structured and systematic approach to quality assurance" (Strandvik 2017: 52).

All the above services and processes ultimately rely on translation expertise for effective implementation. In any holistic approach to translation quality, competence is indeed at the core of quality assurance, together with process and product, as no standard, guideline or assessment grid can be effective without the necessary skills to apply them (see e.g. Prieto Ramos 2015: 20). From this perspective, we will delve into the profiles and challenges of those who are generally responsible for the recruitment and coordination of translation professionals in the pursuit of quality at international organizations: institutional translation service managers (ITSMs), including directors of entire translation services (senior ITSMs) and, in particular, heads or chiefs of language units or sections (mid-level ITSMs or language-bound ITSMs).[1] The aim of this study is to contribute to our understanding of what it takes to be an ITSM today by asking two key questions: What is the role of institutional translation team managers in TQA? What skills are required of them considering global trends in the field?

To this end, the following sections will draw an overview of institutional translation service management based on the combined analysis of: (1) the management structures of 12 organizations (eight intergovernmental and four EU institutions); (2) the job descriptions contained in 14 ITSM vacancy notices (seven for language section chiefs and seven for service directors, randomly selected among vacancies announced at international organizations between 2010 and 2016, including four from EU institutions, two for each level of management); and (3) 24 interviews with mid-level ITSMs (three per language service) conducted in three representative institutional settings between April and July 2017: the EU (more precisely, the European Commission's Directorate-General for Translation (DGT), the Council of the EU, the European Parliament and the Court of Justice of the EU), with 24 official languages; the United Nations (UN), including three of its duty stations, with six official languages; and the World Trade Organization (WTO), with three official languages, an example of medium-size specialized in-

[1]In this chapter, denominations are used in a non-exhaustive way to include all possible titles of comparable structures or profiles. For instance, "translation services" might be part of a "division" or a "department", and be composed of various language "sections", "units" or "departments", depending on the institution. Likewise, "heads" might be called "chiefs" or "directors" at different management levels, while "quality advisers" might be "managers", "coordinators", "controllers" or "focal points" depending on rank and nature of the job in each institution. These arbitrary denominations are secondary to the rationale behind the structures and duties presented in this paper.

tergovernmental institution. In order to focus on commonalities and preserve anonymity, reference to specific organizations is avoided to the extent possible and no individual ITSM is quoted in the presentation of results.

The next section will provide a brief account of the most common responsibilities of ITSMs at international organizations (§2). This account will prepare the ground for a closer exploration of TQA-related practices and challenges of translation unit managers responsible for quality in their respective languages in the three selected institutional settings (§3). These data will inform conclusions regarding ITSMs' and TQA (§4).

2 Institutional translation management duties: the common ground

The responsibilities of ITSMs vary depending on the structures and features of their translation services, which, in turn, reflect institutional approaches to multilingualism. All the services surveyed (12 in total) were established to support the production of legal, policy and administrative documents in a diversity of official languages. They epitomize a hierarchical paradigm in which ITSMs stand at the top and tend to specialize more or less in managerial or translation and revision tasks depending on the size of the service. While the prototypical *management structure* includes at least one director of service and several heads of language units or sections, the largest services (in terms of staff, translation volumes and number of languages) have more complex organigrams and a higher degree of division of management and transversal tasks. The service structure often justifies the delegation of functions such as coordinating thematic projects or monitoring certain aspects of TQA implementation (e.g. in the case of quality managers or advisers at EU institutions). This is explained by the more significant need to coordinate or harmonize policies and practices between, and even within, service units, at times located in different duty stations.

At the other extreme, in very small services, ITSMs may actually be the only in-house staff. This is the case of one small organization included in our sample. The service is composed of one manager per target language (two in total) in charge of outsourcing translations depending on workload fluctuations, as well as translating, revising and managing all aspects of quality assurance. ITSMs deal with a significant concentration of translation and project management functions but have a more modest administrative workload compared to larger services, particularly with regard to human resources.

The most common *duties* of mid-level ITSMs, as found in the structures and vacancy notices examined, can be summarized under four categories, from more strategic to more practical translation work:

- Strategic, administrative and financial matters
- Staffing matters, including recruitment and performance appraisal
- Translation workflow coordination
- Contribution to translation, technical and quality control tasks

All categories are interrelated, particularly categories 1 to 3, as strategic and financial matters are then reflected in implementation aspects supervised under categories 2 and 3, while category 4 tends to vary enormously depending on the size of the service. In larger services, managers are not always expected to revise on a regular basis, and they rarely translate, as opposed to managers of smaller services.

Among the sample job descriptors of mid-level ITSMs, the most detailed one was published by the UN. The responsibilities listed in the relevant vacancy notice are reproduced in Table 1 below and aligned to the four functional categories identified above. This list can be considered representative of management duties at language unit level in large translation services.

The same exercise can be applied to other descriptors. The list of duties in each category will be similar or shorter depending on profile variations and the level of detail provided. For instance, strategic and human resources matters in the above vacancy notice contrast with the short reference to planning, training and guidance in the equivalent vacancy notice at a much smaller agency, the International Atomic Energy Agency, where ITSMs at unit level devote more time to translation and revision tasks (see Table 2 below).

In the same vacancy notice, the role of the section head is previously presented as "a translator and a reviser who is responsible for the overall quality and timeliness" of translations, and "a manager planning and monitoring the work and supervising the staff of the Section"; and the "main purpose" of the position is: "To plan, coordinate and supervise the translation/revision activities of the Section, ensuring the high quality and timely delivery of texts translated into [language] for distribution to Member States and/or members of the Secretariat."

As to directors of entire translation services (or senior ITSMs), the most common functions listed generally fall under category 1 above (strategic, administrative and financial matters) but at a higher level of responsibility. The more managerial profile of these positions is also reflected in the discourse used in the job descriptors. They all include the following core duties: coordination of the various component sections or units, strategic planning and leadership, liaison with other departments and external representation. Most organizations

Table 1: Duties of mid-level ITSM in representative vacancy notice (large service)

1. Strategic, administrative and financial matters
    - participating in the senior management group of the Division and assuming the leadership role on ad hoc task forces or projects as required
    - making recommendations to the Director of the Documentation Division on policy, administrative and operational matters of the Service, including monitoring and highlighting technological advances that could facilitate the work of the Service/Division
    - serving as Officer-in-Charge of the Division when required
    - coordinating long-term meeting coverage with other précis-writing Services
    - preparing reports on all aspects of the Service
2. Staffing matters, including recruitment and performance appraisal
    - making long and short-term projections of the work of the Service and its staffing requirements
    - supervising and monitoring the performance of all staff in the Service and preparing e-Performance reports as First Reporting Officer for the staff directly reporting to the Chiefs and acts as Second Reporting Officer accordingly
    - screening applications from and evaluating potential freelance staff and contractors, and preparing requests for contractual translation or the recruitment of temporary assistance as needed
    - making recommendations on such personnel actions as recruitment, renewal of contracts, transfers, assignments and promotions
    - selecting papers for examinations, marking scripts, establishing pass lists, participating in examination boards and interviews to ensure appropriate recruitment
    - organizing training
3. Translation workflow coordination
    - managing the staff and work programme of the Service to ensure the timely issuance in [language] of documents
    - organizing all activities of the Service to ensure maximum efficiency and cost-effectiveness
    - formulating and developing guidelines, instructions and priorities governing translation, revision, précis writing and terminology work of the Service
    - preparing internal information notes on work procedures
4. Contribution to translation, technical and quality control tasks
    - carrying out quality control checks for work done in-house and by outside contractors
    - serving as the final arbiter on all technical problems connected with the language of the Service
    - translating and/or revising particularly important, sensitive or confidential texts, as required

Table 2: Duties of mid-level ITSM in representative vacancy notice (medium-size service)

• Plan, supervise and monitor the work of the Section and provide training and guidance. • Take authoritative decisions regarding terminology, style and usage in [language]. • Revise the translations done by other members of the Section. • Translate and self-revise texts mainly from English into [language] covering a range of scientific, technical, administrative and legal subjects ensuring that translations are equivalent in meaning and style to the original texts.

surveyed (except for EU institutions) group together all language service departments, including interpreting and other documentation services, under the same management line. The example below (Table 3), a notice published by the WTO in 2016, illustrates the duties of senior ITSMs who manage translation services and other sections within the same division.

A comparison between this notice and the wording used on the same position six years earlier is indicative of recent management trends in the field, with more explicit references to notions of cost-effectiveness and streamlining of practices. For instance, "work to *refine policies, systems and processes* so as to *maximise quality, efficiency and value for money*" (our emphasis) in point 4 replaces the following wording in the 2010 notice: "Manage and ensure *continuous improvement / modernization of the operations* in all areas of the Division, *ensuring a high level of efficiency, service orientation and quality*" (our emphasis).

With regard to quality, as in the above examples, the other job descriptions of mid-level and senior ITSMs (except for two in the second group) refer to translation quality in formulations such as "ensure quality / quality control", "meet required quality standards" and "set standards for translation quality assurance". Overall, these formulations tend to refer to overarching policy aspects in the case of senior ITSMs, as opposed to more technical implementation and monitoring aspects in the case of mid-level ITSMs. As managers responsible for everyday decisions on quality assurance in their respective languages, the latter will be the focus of the next section.

Table 3: Duties of senior ITSM in representative vacancy notice

1. Manage the operations of the Division to provide language, documentation and information management services in alignment with the needs of the Secretariat and Members. To this end refine and implement a Divisional strategy and relevant policies as necessary.

2. Achieve annual service targets and ensure the Division performs within budget (ca. 28 million CHF per annum) obtaining efficiency gains and bringing costs into line with international standards and market considerations.

3. Lead, motivate and provide guidance to line managers. Establish their responsibilities and performance objectives for his/her direct reports, provide feedback on their performance and implement any changes required. Build the divisional team, developing their potential ensuring they are trained as required and providing leadership by setting standards.

4. Establish a culture of continuous improvement in the Division and work to refine policies, systems and processes so as to maximise quality, efficiency and value for money.

5. Ensure collaboration with other Divisions and provide contributions to their work as necessary.

6. Represent the WTO Secretariat in various events in Geneva and abroad that address matters related to the work of the Division, including speaking engagements.

7. Support the Director-General and Senior Management by providing reports, briefings and other information and advice as required.

3 Translation unit heads and TQA: practices and challenges

What lies behind the descriptors of ITSMs' duties in terms of practical TQA? To what extent may they have a real impact on translation quality? In order to complete the overview of TQA operations among ITSMs, we will examine the reported practices of those in charge of monitoring TQA implementation by language, i.e. language unit heads or mid-level ITSMs, at three representative institutional settings: the EU, the UN and the WTO. For the sake of comparability, heads of unit of three official languages common to the three settings (English, French and Spanish) were interviewed,[2] up to a total of 24 language unit heads. The primary aim was to provide a snapshot of common practices and challenges on the basis of data compiled through open-ended questions in structured interviews on working procedures, with a focus on quality assurance.

Quality managers and advisers (who support the coordination of quality matters at the EU institutions) and service directors were also interviewed in the context of a larger project on institutional translation quality.[3] The replies of these professionals were very useful: (1) to triangulate and better understand the information on institutional structures and management duties presented in the previous section; (2) to confirm that strategic and policy aspects of TQA are generally perceived by service directors as the collective responsibility of translation units in each language, with the peculiarity of more visible strategic support and coordination by quality advisers in the case of the EU institutions; and (3) to corroborate the relevance of focusing on language unit heads as the most comparable and comprehensive decision-making profile among the institutions in terms of everyday TQA implementation. In this respect, it must also be noted that this section reports on their practices and perceptions, but does not purport to assess TQA approaches, which falls outside the scope of the present study.

In analyzing TQA-related activities of mid-level ITSMs, the first important commonality is that they all bear the *responsibility* and are accountable for the quality of translation in their respective target languages, and they are all conditioned by institutional goals and working procedures. They are not bound by any shared international standard, as ISO 17100:2015 would require a policy of systematic full revision that does not apply to their services. Many managers were not acquainted with this new standard, which does not actually describe the tasks and qualification requirements of service managers themselves. However, ISO 17100:2015 on "Translation services – Requirements for translation services" establishes the "actions necessary for the delivery of a quality translation service" by TSPs, including provisions "concerning the management of core processes, minimum qualification requirements, the availability and management of resources, and other actions" (ISO 17100:2015 2015: vi). It is therefore implied that the role of managers of TSPs is to make sure that the specified measures are taken with a view to delivering a quality product. It also follows that ISO 17100:2015 provides a useful yardstick to compare TQA tasks in institutional settings and to

[2]For logistical reasons, one of them was replaced *ad interim*.

[3]"Legal Translation in International Institutional Settings: Scope, Strategies and Quality Markers (LETRINT)".

employ standardized terminology in the field. In fact, this international standard is explicitly quoted as a key source in the quality *guidelines* of one EU institution in particular.[4]

The shift towards more explicit principles and frameworks was also confirmed at other EU institutions, while it was not felt as a compelling necessity in intergovernmental organizations with fewer languages. In these cases, the core TQA principles were primarily based on well-established practices as gradually inherited and adapted to changing needs. Whether driven by custom or formal guidelines, the *discretionary margin* of all language unit heads was conditioned by shared core principles. Within this margin, *implementation variations per language* were noticeable in all institutions, although they were almost negligible in the service with the smallest number of languages. These variations reflected not only different unit backgrounds and working approaches, but also, at times, more pro-active managerial attitudes towards TQA procedures and supporting tools.

Mid-level ITSMs were involved in the following *TQA-related tasks* to varying degrees, depending on structures and workload fluctuations. Table 4 below classifies the data compiled during the interviews in an attempt to draw an up-to-date structured inventory. While some of the tasks can be facilitated by computer applications (e.g. translation management tools), partially delegated within a language unit (e.g. follow-up of quality checks, job assignments or specific project management) or centralized by a separate dedicated unit (e.g. contracting operations), language unit managers are ultimately the orchestra conductors with a full overview of, and the capacity to influence, the different components of TQA in each language in which quality is measured. As evidenced by a comparison between the inventory below (Table 4) and Table 1, most of the responsibilities listed in their job descriptors actually have a TQA dimension. From this per-

[4]In connection with general quality criteria, *DGT Translation Quality Guidelines* establish that: "All translated texts should comply with the general principles and quality requirements for professional translation laid down in the international standard ISO 17100" (DGT 2015: 3). The criteria contained in ISO provision 5.3.1 (ISO 17100:2015 2015: 10) are then listed in a footnote:

> a) compliance with specific domain and client terminology and/or any other reference material provided and ensuring terminological consistency during translation; b) semantic accuracy of the target language content; c) appropriate syntax, spelling, punctuation, diacritical marks, and other orthographical conventions of the target language; d) lexical cohesion and phraseology; e) compliance with any proprietary and/or client style guide (including domain, language register, and language variants); f) locale and any applicable standards; g) formatting; h) target audience and purpose of the target language content.

Table 4: TQA-related tasks of mid-level ITSMs

I. PRODUCTION WORKFLOW SUPERVISION

a) Overall planning and coordination

- Planning and team coordination according to budget targets, deadlines, priorities and available human resources; contingency plans and problem-solving in case of unexpected changes in programme or project implementation.
- Communication with requesting units, other translation units, support units (such as technology, terminology or documentation) or any other relevant actors where appropriate to meet targets.

b) Job categorization and assignment

- Translation brief processing and, where appropriate, clarification of specifications or discussion of conditions with requesting unit.
- Content profiling and risk assessment: text categorization according to text type within institutional hierarchy, subject matters, sensitivity and confidentiality; definition of expected level of quality; potential impact of lower-than-expected quality.
- Assignment of job to translator: best possible match between text and translator profile (specialization, in-house / external, speed, etc.) depending on availability of human resources, risk assessment and time constraints.
- Assignment of job to quality controller[a] (except for cases of self-revised translation): type and level of quality control (full bilingual revision, monolingual target text checks or review, etc.) considering the two previous points; best possible match with quality controller profile depending on quality control needs, availability of human resources and time constraints.

c) Monitoring of quality assessment and handling of feedback

- Monitoring of compliance with quality assessment procedures: mandatory for external translators (criteria generally harmonized for all units); more or less systematic and detailed depending on language unit and translator rank or seniority in the case of in-house translators.
- Supervision of ex-post quality checks at unit level.
- Processing of feedback on production and satisfaction survey results.

[a]This term is used in a broad sense to refer to the person who conducts any quality control task (see e.g. Mossop 2014: 116), regardless of the institutional category held by the person. In EU institutions, for example, revision practices are not as hierarchically organized as in the other two selected settings, and in-house translators are usually expected to translate and revise from their very entry into the position.

II. CONTRIBUTION TO TRANSLATION, QUALITY CONTROL OR ASSESSMENT TASKS

- Contribution to quality control or, less often, translation tasks in specific projects (e.g. texts of highest importance).
- Regular or random assessment of translation or quality control output.
- Advice and arbitration on linguistic issues where appropriate (e.g. cases of internal disagreement or sensitive institutional terminology).

III. COMPETENCE MANAGEMENT

- Participation in recruitment tests and selection of applicants.
- Individual goal-setting and periodic performance appraisal exercises with members of staff.
- Training initiatives in line with team and individual competence development needs.
- Mentoring coordination for junior staff members.

IV. RESOURCE DEVELOPMENT AND CONTRIBUTION TO INSTITUTIONAL TQA POLICY

- Resource needs analysis and monitoring of language-specific resource development, including cooperation with terminology units or focal points.
- Transmission of feedback on tools and resources for potential improvements at a broader level.
- Monitoring of impact of management measures and reporting on unit level quality developments.
- Contribution to TQA policy formulation or implementation innovations that may be exported to other units.

spective, mid-level ITSMs play a central role in promoting quality, especially as *process and competence managers.* In the case of regular contributions to quality control as revisers (category II tasks), particularly common in smaller services, the short-term impact on the translation product can be more direct. However, the *long-term impact* of ITSMs on translation product quality as TQA managers crucially depends on the cumulative effect of the other three elements of a virtuous circle: (1) competence management (selection of talent and professional development actions under category III); (2) workflow supervision (category I tasks) with a view to maximizing the benefits of competence assets in the production process; and (3) input into procedural and material conditions that may improve workflow and performance (category IV actions).

The degree of risk in job assignment is directly related to the degree of suitability and reliability of team members, so administering talent and keeping motivation high, despite productivity pressures, emerges as a key requirement for effective TQA management in hierarchical institutional structures. By the same token, adapting selection processes to competence needs can only be a sound quality enhancement investment.

Unsurprisingly, any measures that introduce uncertainty in job allocation equations or other links of the production chain feature as the most common concern among mid-level ITSMs with regard to TQA. The main **challenges** identified revolve around three interrelated sources of uncertainty:

- *Resource availability and productivity pressures* as a result of streamlining or downsizing: translation services are regularly in the spotlight given the proportion of institutional budgets they represent; as in any other public or private sector, it is generally felt that insufficient resources could lead to lower-than-expected quality outcomes if the limits of cost-effectiveness are exceeded.

- *External contracting conditions*: in light of the increasing level of outsourced translation, it has become paramount to build professional relations of trust and promote quality among external translators; in institutions where outsourcing procedures prevent language units from matching job specifications to individual translator profiles, and jobs are assigned by external contractors, the translator's reliability is generally unknown by ITSMs, so the risk assessment and production chain can be affected as a result (including greater unpredictability of quality control needs, impact on motivation and human resource allocation in cases of lower-than-expected quality of outsourced translation, and final cost/quality ratio).

- *Workflow changes and expectations deriving from technological developments*: the integration of new tools is perceived as globally positive in supporting and speeding up certain tasks, but has also brought new variables and dependencies into the workflow, as well as new error patterns in the production process; in this connection, heightened expectations of the benefits of machine translation and over-simplification of badly-needed human translation expertise represent an added challenge in the context of cost-saving initiatives.

Other challenges fall outside the decision-making scope of language units (in particular, the persistent issue of poor quality of originals) or were specific to certain units, for example, the complexity of managing a high number of language pairs and finding available translators in some of them, or insufficient adaptation of initial screening exercises to professional translation profiles in some recruitment processes.

4 Concluding remarks: expertise for evolving TQA management

The insights gathered in previous sections point to the skills expected of ITSMs at language unit level from a holistic TQA perspective. ISO 17100:2015 does not refer to the profile of service managers but to TSP project managers, who are required to have "appropriate translation project management competence" (ISO 17100:2015 2015: 7). As outlined above, mid-level ITSMs are crucial decision-makers in sustained TQA endeavours beyond translation project level. Their services can be equated to those of TSP branches in the private sector, but conditioned by specific institutional goals and conventions.

In their capacity as competence and process managers, an optimal combination of translation expertise and managerial skills would be expected of these mid-level ITSMs, particularly in connection with the textual and extra-textual parameters considered in resource allocation. As noted by Gouadec (2010: 275), quality management systems require "a very clear view of "product" quality grades and levels, overall, per domain, per parameter, and per sub-parameters". In international institutional settings, this relates to established text categories, legal hierarchies and priority policy matters that constitute essential knowledge for TQA managers. As team leaders in the provision of and advocacy for translation quality in the relevant language, they would also be expected to have advanced translation and revision skills, as well as sufficient expertise in TQA processes (including approaches to quality control and evaluation), translation competence development, and translation tools and resources. The ideal ITSM profile also demands general management skills such as planning, coordination, risk management and networking abilities.

The appropriate balance between translation and management skills will depend on the degree to which translation and revision work or other routine operations are delegated from ITSMs in each organization. What seems clear in all the settings analyzed is that the shift from one-fits-all quality control to a more modulated approach to quality variables has made ITSMs' role more critical and influential in TQA. In light of the growing prominence of external and machine assisted translation, it is also clear that TQA management functions and their impact deserve further attention. As the translation landscape continues to evolve rapidly, the sophistication and added value of this profile will certainly evolve as well. To the extent that international organizations renew their commitment to quality multilingual communication, TQA managers are called to play a central role in promoting effective solutions at the intersection between top-down processes of policy implementation and bottom-up input for quality enhancement.

Acknowledgements

I would like to thank all institutional partners for their valuable cooperation, as well as the Swiss National Science Foundation for its support through a Consolidator Grant.

References

Canfora, Carmen & Angelika Ottmann. 2015. Risikomanagement für Übersetzungen. *Trans-kom* 8(2). 314–346.

Directorate-General for Translation (DGT), European Commission. 2015. *DGT translation quality guidelines.* http://ec.europa.eu/translation/maltese/guidelines/documents/dgt_translation_quality_guidelines_en.pdf, accessed 2017-8-24.

Drugan, Joanna. 2013. *Quality in professional translation: assessment and improvement.* London: Bloomsbury.

Dunne, Elena S. 2013. *Project risk management: Developing a risk framework for translation projects.* Kent State University dissertation. https://etd.ohiolink.edu/rws_etd/document/get/kent1368700402/inline, accessed 2017-11-14.

Fields, Paul, Daryl Hague, Geoffrey S. Koby, Arle Lommel & Alan Melby. 2014. What is quality? A management discipline and the translation industry get acquainted. *Tradumàtica* 12. 404–412.

García, Ignacio. 2015. Cloud marketplaces: procurement of translators in the age of social media. *Journal of Specialised Translation* 23. 18–38.

Görög, Attila. 2014. Translation and quality: Editorial. *Tradumàtica* 12. 388–391.

Gouadec, Daniel. 2010. Quality in translation. In Yves Gambier & van Doorslaer Luc (eds.), *Handbook of Translation Studies*, vol. 1, 270–275. Amsterdam: John Benjamins.

ISO 17100:2015. 2015. *Translation services – Requirements for translation services.* Geneva: ISO. http://www.iso.org/iso/catalogue_detail.htm?csnumber=59149.

Jiménez-Crespo, Miguel A. 2017. How much would you like to pay? reframing and expanding the notion of translation quality through crowdsourcing and volunteer approaches. *Perspectives. Studies in Translation Theory and Practice* 25(3). 478–491. DOI:10.1080/0907676X.2017.1285948

Mossop, Brian. 2014. *Revising and editing for translators.* 3rd edn. London: Routledge.

O'Brien, Sharon. 2012. Towards a dynamic quality evaluation model for translation. *Journal of Specialised Translation* 17. 55–77.

Prieto Ramos, Fernando. 2015. Quality assurance in legal translation: evaluating process, competence and product in the pursuit of adequacy. *International Journal for the Semiotics of Law* 28. 11–30.

Prioux, René & Michel Rochard. 2007. Économie de la révision dans une organisation internationale : le cas de l'OCDE. *Journal of Specialised Translation* 8. 21–41.

for Standardization (CEN), European Committee. 2006. *EN 15038:2006 Translation services – service requirements.* Brussels: CEN.

Strandvik, Ingemar. 2017. Towards a more structured approach to quality assurance: DGT's quality journey. In Fernando Prieto Ramos (ed.), *Institutional translation for international governance: enhancing quality in multilingual legal communication*, 51–62. London: Bloomsbury.

Wright, Sue Ellen. 2006. Language industry standards. In Keiran J. Dunne (ed.), *Perspectives on localization*, 241–278. Amsterdam: John Benjamins.

Chapter 5

Translation manuals and style guides as quality assurance indicators: The case of the European Commission's Directorate-General for Translation

Tomáš Svoboda
Charles University, Prague

The aim of this chapter is to verify the assumption that institutional translation on the supranational level is, by definition, concerned primarily with terminology, style guides, that it is standardized, and its quality aspect is governed by rules (cf. Koskinen 2008, Schäffner et al. 2014). It will concentrate on translation manuals and style guides, since extensive studies on this topic seem to have been missing from academic research. To fill this gap as regards inquiries into the workings of one particular (EU) institution, this chapter presents the results of research into translation manuals and style guides used by and within the European Commission's Directorate-General for Translation (DGT). The DGT on-line collection of guidelines (referred to as the Resources website here), which primarily offers materials to DGT contractors, represents arguably the most extensive and most complex translation resource ever compiled. The present research is based on empirical data: as of the time of the study (the first half of 2017), a total of 793 links to individual translation manuals and style guides were included in a research corpus encompassing all the 24 official languages of the EU. The information was surveyed using a blend of quantitative and qualitative approaches. As for the results, the extensiveness of the DGT reference material could be shown together with its linkages to the translation quality aspect, whether these are explicit or implicit. As regards the structure of the resources, an overall top-down standardization approach could be proven, although, at the same time, the resources show a certain degree of variation. The following areas were identified as being the crucial requirements DGT has vis-à-vis its contractors: references to EU institutions and DGT departments, binding terminology resources and the Interinstitutional Style Guide.

Tomáš Svoboda. 2017. Translation manuals and style guides as quality assurance indicators: The case of the European Commission's Directorate-General for Translation. In Tomáš Svoboda, Łucja Biel & Krzysztof Łoboda (eds.), *Quality aspects in institutional translation*, 75–107. Berlin: Language Science Press. DOI:10.5281/zenodo.1048190

1 Introduction

It has been shown for the European Commission's Directorate-General for Translation (DGT) that there is enormous divergence among language departments both in the topics covered by translation manuals (TMs) and style guides (SGs) as well as in the level of detail of such resources.[1] Research so far (cf. §2 below) has analyzed just a handful of individual guidelines and there has been no inquiry into the overall pool of the SGs and TMs used by and within DGT – in fact, Felipe Boto & Antolín (2009: 56) have made an explicit remark ("we must lament") that little use is made of the material provided by the translation services of EU institutions. To gain a clearer understanding of the wealth of "house memory" in DGT (which, according to DGT's own information and relevant literature, is the largest translation department in an institutional setting in the world) and of its relation to quality management,[2] a study of the DGT Resource website entitled "Guidelines for translation contractors"[3] has been performed. It has yielded a comprehensive account as to the structure (logical organization) of how the SGs/TMs are presented, the types and nature of the resources, and their linkage to the overall quality assurance goal of the service. The current research findings can be of relevance both to the field of institutional translation within Translation Studies (as it contributes to the understanding of the specificities of the former within the discipline more generally) and to practice, since the findings offer insights into a set of materials that are aimed at translation service providers/translation contractors.

2 State of the art in studying style guides and translation manuals

The notion of rules is constitutive to the concept of institutional translation (cf., e.g., Koskinen 2008: 18, Halverson 2008: 343, Kang 2009: 142 and in a less straightforward way Becker-Mrotzek 1990: 159). Various types of "rules" have been de-

[1]Topics range from terminology to workflow rules and SG/TM volumes range from one-page materials to a manifold of that. For example, the German in-house style guide featured 690 pages in mid-2017; it was 1,009 pages long in 2013, cf. Svoboda (2013).

[2]For a discussion on the terms such as QM, QA, cf. mainly Biel; Strandvik, and Vandepitte, in this volume. A recent and very relevant source in this context is Prieto Ramos (2017). Further discussion of the terms by the author of this chapter can be found in Svoboda (forthcoming).

[3]Available from: https://ec.europa.eu/info/resources-partners/translation-and-drafting-resources/guidelines-translation-contractors_en (Accessed 2017-8-30).

scribed or mentioned in the literature so far.[4] In an interesting account, Ian Mason's seminal text (Mason 2004 [2003]) lists the reasons for issuing guidelines to govern the translation practice: they are in place either because they have been issued to the translators by the institution (e.g., glossaries, style guides, codes of practice) or as a result of a "development which grows over a period of years out of shared experience, the need to find common approaches to recurring problems or through advice and training offered to new employees" (2004 [2003]: 470).

One explicit linkage between translation (product/process) quality and SGs/TMs has been suggested by Sosoni (in the context of translator training and the future roles of translation students as contractors for EU institutions): "[...] translation quality is inextricably related to the reliable implementation of the guidelines set out by the EU institutions" (2011: 100). Another overlap of the two concepts of SGs/TMs and translation quality can be found in a document issued by the European Commission's DGT (2012: 17). This publication sees the ultimate role of style guides at the pre-translation stage: "Quality in translation in the stage before translation corresponds to prevention of poor quality and includes recruitment, training, terminology, style guides, etc.; during translation, quality is a matter of choosing the right translator for the job...". This view obviously approaches quality from the point of view of quality assurance (QA). Consequently, by the statement "Quality in translation [...] includes [...] style guides" it means, most likely, that ensuring product quality involves preliminary investment in QA tools, such as SGs. Otherwise, a look at the SGs/TMs made available by the Commission's own DGT reveals that they cover everything from how to deal best with searches, how to perform editing work, how to send translations and, eventually, to how the billing procedure works, etc., which means that all the phases of the translation process are covered by SGs/TMs[5], not just the preliminary stage. Most recently, Drugan et al. (2018) deal with the quality aspect in EU institutions, covering the topic of guidelines to the same extent as well. Strandvik (2017b) is an equally recent study, which devotes several passages to TMs and SGs specifically in the context of DGT translation services and the pertinent QM framework.

An analysis of a particular style guide, specifically the EU *Interinstitutional Style Guide*, may be found in Svoboda (2013). The paper also examines the workflow at the DGT, linking it with the question of what style guides and transla-

[4]For example, established procedures, explicit principles, glossaries, guidance, (written and unwritten) guidelines, guides, guiding principles, institutional 'group mind', institutional doctrines, instructions, manuals, norms, official guidance on (translation) policy, organized procedures, style guides, terminology requirements, translator's handbooks, algorithms (e.g., automatic TM analysis, pre-translation), codes of practice, (EU) culture, customs, etc.

[5]For a more detailed discussion, see Svoboda 2008.

tion guidelines are pertinent to what stages of the translation process. It also presents results of a brief analysis of a sample of guidelines for the DGT translation contractors. Apart from the study results, the paper also gives an extended bibliography overview on the topic of SGs and TMs.

Whereas it is generally assumed that guidelines are an organic part of a translating institution's practice, this assumption calls for refinement when different types of institutions are compared. For example, it has been established in national contexts (in a comparison of EU countries' central government bodies) that "best practice is hardly ever recorded in translation manuals and house style codes are rather an exception" (Svoboda forthcoming). Such findings contradict the common notion of quality assurance in institutional settings, since it was coined based on the top-level (supranational and/or international) translating institutions.

Typically, the aim of guidelines is to improve the product quality of the delivered texts and ultimately to save time and resources on the part of the translating institution, including avoiding extensive revision work. The guiding principle behind a manual is not always explicitly stated in the SGs/TMs themselves. As one of the exceptions, the EU *Guide for external translators* makes the following statement:

> Its main aim is to provide the contractors with practical information to help them with the translation work assigned by the DGT and to facilitate the communication between the contractors and the Commission (DGT's Language departments and External Translation Unit), by laying down certain rules for standardization (word-processing software, layout) and for the use of information technology. (DGT 2008: 4).

Another study authored by the European Commission's DGT (2013: 175–186) gives results of an informative survey on the availability/unavailability of SGs in the drafting process in various international organizations. Although this material is not primarily aimed at translators, some important observations of a more widely applicable nature are made here as regards the extent to which guidelines are used: "Guidelines may not solve all possible problems [...] Instructions tend to overlap [...] [There is] concern [...] about the streamlining of instructions issued. A constant reminder [...] is that too many instructions can fail in their purpose, and simply be ignored by drafters" (2013: 175).

Kaisa Koskinen (2011) refers to guidelines as she links them with standardization and other frequently occurring features of institutional translation, i.e. its collective and anonymous nature. Besides guidelines, she adds, contemporary institutions use databases, term banks and CAT tools (cf. Koskinen 2011: 58). She concludes her article by stating that "customs and [...] guidelines [related to institutions and institutional translation] are in no way uniform [among various types of institutions ...]. Understanding institutional translation [...] requires [...] detailed case studies of different institutional contexts. This research has only just begun in Translation Studies." (Koskinen 2011: 59) The author of this chapter shares Koskinen's view and presents his research as a contribution to fill these blind spots for one particular institution (i.e. DGT).

3 Methodology

In order to obtain the necessary data for describing the DGT Resource website[6] in a comprehensive manner as regards its surface representation, both quantitative and qualitative methods were applied, with a focus on the former.

Using a quantitative approach, 24 individual webpages, which constitute the DGT Resources website,[7] were surveyed in terms of the overlap and divergence of the material presented. To this end, the relevant material per language was copied into a specific table, with hyperlinks preserved.[8] Then the 24 individual tables were collated to form one comprehensive table representing the collection of the entire material available on the Resources website. This represents the actual research corpus, containing 793 links to individual SGs/TMs of all the 24 language departments.[9] Afterwards, in a qualitatively informed matching exercise, clusters of similar information across the language specific webpages were identified and labelled 'categories' for the purposes of our study. Thus, the content of all the pages was cross-checked against the availability or absence of the same or similar categories on other webpages. Typically, any two identical pieces of information contained in any two webpages formed the basis for creating a specific category. The results of this part are presented in §4.3.

Using a qualitative method, then, the information carried by the actual hyperlinks was studied in detail with the aim of obtaining knowledge of the target sites/pages/files as referenced by the DGT resources hub. Domains, keywords, and expressions that are contained in the links as well as the surface text rep-

[6]A distinction is made between a website and a webpage. A website is a superordinate term referring to a bundle or a structure of webpages.

[7]Guidelines for translation contractors, referred to as the "Resources website" here. For the actual analysis of the webpage, see §4.

[8]All links were copied on 2017-6-30.

[9]Individual link text was summarized, i.e. only text appearing as the (active) hyperlink, not accompanying (inactive) description texts. Owing to limits to this research, the linked resources were neither actually retrieved, nor analyzed in terms of their content.

resentation of the links were surveyed and analyzed with special attention paid to the translation quality aspect, in order to fulfil the initial aim of studying the linkages between DGT styleguides and translation quality. The results of this research phase are given below, in §4.4.

Finally, given the fact that this area of institutional translation (i.e. TMs/SGs) was the subject of a pilot study using a limited research corpus in 2013,[10] data will be presented to draw comparisons between the 2013 research and this chapter, which takes a more extensive approach.

Altogether, this chapter examines the below listed main assumptions. Their choice is governed by two main objectives: (i) Prior research has identified some features which are supposed to apply to institutional translation, however, due to limited research conducted so far, it is difficult to confirm whether and to what extent they apply to specific institution types (cf., e.g., TMs and SGs in national contexts). In this respect, the present research is a contribution to testing the validity of previous claims on a particular institution (i.e. DGT). (ii) The below assumptions have been chosen due to the fact that they address the core area of interest here, i.e. the examination of SGs/TMs as quality assurance indicators:

- **Institutional translation** is a field characterized by **standardization**[11] (Koskinen 2011: 58).

- Despite the validity of hypothesis no. 1, the **amount and the nature of references** used as part of the translator resources will **differ among Resource pages.**[12]

- As regards the content of the material researched, it is expected to relate to **reference materials, terminology, style/style guides** (cf. Koskinen 2008, Schäffner et al. 2014) as these items have been identified as the most usual candidates for standardization/regulation.

- The **quality** aspect of institutional translation is governed by **rules.**

[10] Cf. Svoboda 2013.

[11] This statement seems too obvious to offer the potential of yielding some new findings. However, it remains to be proven what kind of standardization actually applies to individual institutions, such as the DGT here.

[12] This hypothesis is based on the outcomes of a pilot study, cf. Svoboda (2013).

4 Analysis of the DGT's Resources website

As the purpose of this chapter is to analyze the Resource website of the Directorate-General for Translation of the European Commission both in general and in terms of quality management, the following structure has been chosen for the analytical section. First, the location and structure of the Resource website is shown. Secondly, a quantitative overview of the resources is presented. This part is followed by an analysis of the content (the topics) of the individual resources. Afterwards, link texts of the hyperlinks that were included in the research corpus (i.e. a collection of the references – 793 links, representing the entire material available on the Resources website) are analyzed in detail. Finally, results are projected against the topic of quality management.

4.1 Location, structure and overall description

The Resources website is accessible from the DGT homepage, under Related links (final reference in the side-bar, bottom left; cf. a current screenshot in Figure 1 below) and, subsequently, Translation and drafting resources (second item in the list), and Guidelines for translation contractors. The DGT website and its individual webpages are lean and touchscreen/mobile device optimized (in line with a recent overhaul of the Commission's website Europa.eu).

Once the Resources website is displayed, it comes with a homogenous structure of 24 sections,[13] each representing "useful resources for translations on EU matters", i.e. guidelines for contractors translating into one of the 24 EU official languages featured (see a screenshot in Figure 2 below).

In terms of their actual web address, the resources, after an overhaul of the EU's official europa.eu website,[14] are no longer featured directly as part of the DGT site, but under "Resources for partners", which is directly subsumed to "European Commission" and its Info sub-site (cf. the address as depicted in the command line of Figure 2). This hub page is available in English only and not even in the procedural languages.

The potential recipients of these resources are primarily DGT contractors, i.e. the materials pertain to the outsourcing aspect of DGT work. The outsourced

[13] It needs to be borne in mind that, presumably, a typical user hardly ever ventures to discover the information contained in more than two or three language specific sites. This means that for them, it may never have occurred how vast the entire resource is.

[14] Cf. the "Commission's new web presence" strategy, in which DGT is directly involved: "Work on the new web presence is led by the Commission's communication, translation and IT departments" (https://ec.europa.eu/info/about-commissions-new-web-presence_en (Accessed 2017-6-30)).

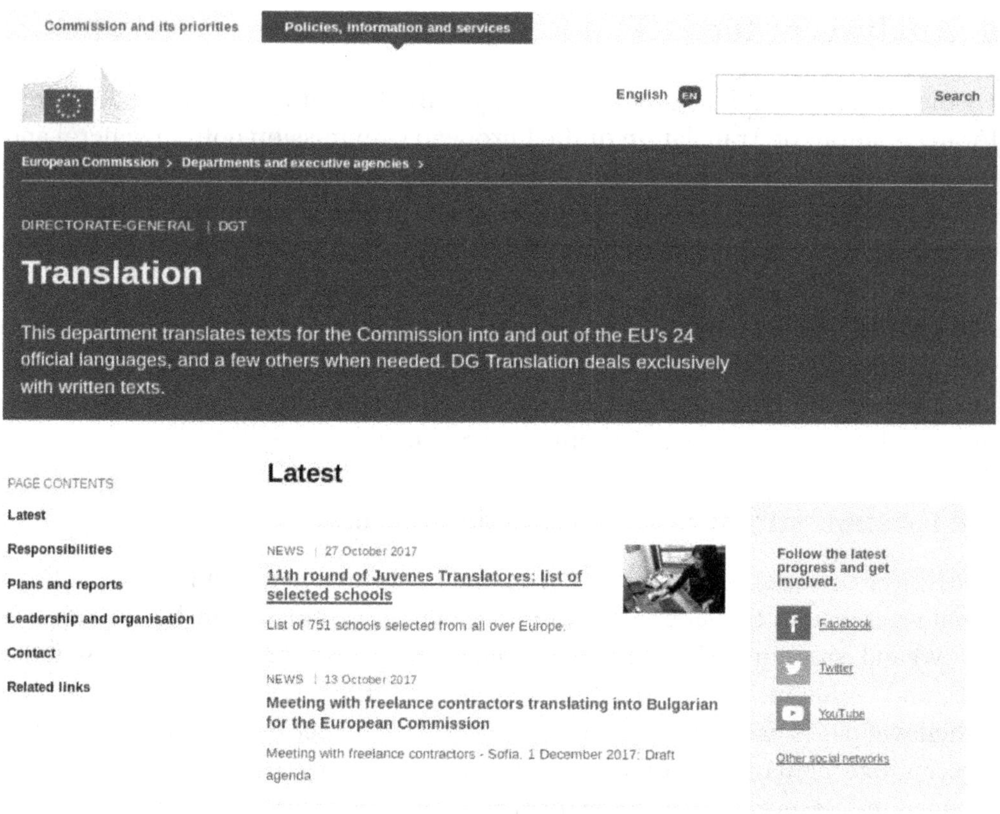

Figure 1: DGT homepage, available from: https://ec.europa.eu/info/departments/translation_en and the Related links reference, bottom left (Accessed 2017-11-22)

production is part of institutional translation, because, in the end, the DGT eventually approves the translations and assumes responsibility for them. Yet even in-house translators do use these resources.[15] What has changed, however, since the recent (Europa website and, consequently) DGT website overhaul, is the fact that the resources section is no longer divided into two main areas. There used to be an intermediary page channeling users according to the translation direction: You chose either the "I translate into [language]" link, or that entitled "I translate out of [language]". The latter section seems to have disappeared from the current

[15]From personal experience (the author of this chapter worked as an in-house DGT translator in Luxembourg for three years after the Czech Republic joined the EU in 2004), I know that apart from the SGs/TMs targeting contractors, there are official SGs/TMs for internal use only (stored within the EC firewall), as well as individual/personal ones of an unofficial nature, created by members of staff for their personal use.

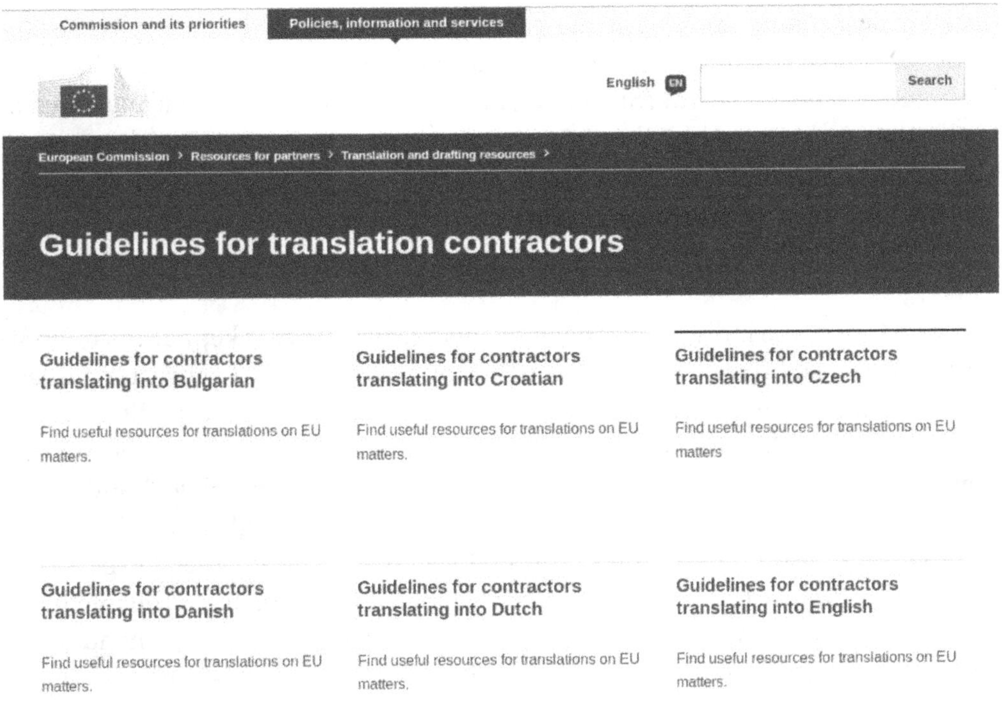

Figure 2: DGT "Guidelines for translation contractors" site, upper part; available from: https://ec.europa.eu/info/resources-partners/translation-and-drafting-resources/guidelines-translation-contractors_en (Accessed 2017-10-10)

Resources website, thus reducing the overall number of resource materials substantially.

In terms of origin, the materials can either be unique to a given language department or derived (translated and/or adapted) from a common source. They are topic and/or media specific and can assume various data formats.

4.2 Quantitative overview of the resources

It was possible to identify language departments with quantitatively the most and eventually the least number of resources. The ultimate champion in terms of the highest number of resources is the Lithuanian one with some 71 items on the webpage, followed by the Swedish with 70 such linked materials. Then, following behind by a distance of more than 20 items, there are just two pages showing in the 50–60 category: the Romanian and the Italian with 52 and 51 sources available, respectively. In the 40–50 tier, there is the Bulgarian, whereas in the 30–40 band there are the Estonian, Danish, Czech, Croatian, Spanish and German ones (listed in descending order). The most frequently represented category is the 20–30 tier (with the following 10 language pages represented in this band): Latvian, Portuguese, Maltese, Slovak, Slovenian, English, Irish, French, Greek and Finnish. Under the 20-hit threshold, there are the Hungarian, Dutch and Polish pages.

4.3 The content of individual pages

4.3.1 The structure of the webpages

The structure of the individual, language-specific webpages is kept uniform, comprising three main sections: (I) "General EU information", (II) "Contractor guides", and (III) "Language-specific information". The first section is further divided into two subsections ("EU institutions", and "European legislation"), the second section is divided into three subsections ("Guidelines", "EU terminology", and "Style guides") and the third section is the same ("Terminology and glossaries", "Models and templates", and "Useful links (national legislation / authorities / expert bodies)"). The individual pages are all presented in English, which, on the one hand makes comparison much easier for the researcher but, on the other hand, however, this is a witness to the presumption that all users are sufficiently proficient in the language, which might be debatable.

Whereas, under Section I and II, the subsections are the same with all 24 webpages, the picture differs in Section III as several pages present only two, one or none of the headings that are common in the majority of the other pages. For example, the subsection "Terminology and glossaries" occurs in 21 out of the 24 pages, whereas the last of the three subheadings ("Useful links [...]") appears in only 13 cases. Only one page (NL) does not feature any of the three subheadings in Section III, whereas 13 pages show all of them.

See Figure 3 for a screenshot of what a typical Resource page looks like.

Tables 1–3 contain a graphic representation of the pages and their content. Tiles with language codes refer to items that are available on the webpage. There are main sections (I.-III. marked as headings in the descriptions to Tables 1–1 below), subsections (headings in bold) and categories (rows with their descriptions, clustered to form subsections). Categories summarize sources that occur twice or more times across the language versions of the Resource pages. The triangle (▲) reference means that there are other resources available that are unique, i.e. they are not repeated across the Resource pages (one triangle mark can represent several unique resources). The order of topics as depicted in the tables reflects the order of TMs/SGs as they appear in the individual webpages. Empty spaces indicate the absence of a specific item (i.e. Not Available).

Guidelines for contractors translating into Czech

Departments Translation

PAGE CONTENTS

General EU information

Contractor guides

Language-specific information

General EU information

EU institutions

- Names of institutions, bodies and agencies of the European Union
- List of directorates-general and departments of the European Commission

European legislation

- EUR-Lex — EU law currently in force
  - Treaties
- Legislative procedures
- Interinstitutional Agreement of 2 December 2013 between the European Parliament, the Council and the Commission on budgetary discipline, on cooperation in budgetary matters and on sound financial management
- Financial regulation and rules of application

Contractor guides

Guidelines

- Guide for contractors translating for the European Commission
- Translation checklist
- Commission document codes (COM, SEC, final, etc.) — rules

EU terminology

- IATE — EU terminology database
- TARIC codes — online customs tariff database
- EU Budget Online
- Eurovoc — multilingual thesaurus covering EU policy fields
- RAMON — Eurostat's statistical metadata website (including combined nomenclature)

Figure 3: DGT "Guidelines for contractors translating into Czech" site, upper part; available from: https://ec.europa.eu/info/resources-partners/translation-and-drafting-resources/guidelines-translation-contractors/guidelines-contractors-translating-czech_en (Accessed 2017-10-10)

Table 1: A comparison of DGT webpages entitled "Guidelines for contractors translating into [LANGUAGE]", Section I. General EU information. Available from: https://ec.europa.eu/info/resources-partners/translation-and-drafting-resources/guidelines-translation-contractors_en (Accessed 2017-6-30)

	BG	HR	CS	DA	NL	EN	ET	FI	FR	DE	EL	HU	IT	GA	LV	LT	MT	PL	PT	RO	SK	SL	ES	SV
EU institutions																								
Names of institutions, bodies and agencies of the EU	BG	HR	CS	DA	NL	EN	ET	FI	FR	DE	EL	HU	IT	GA	LV	LT	MT	PL	PT	RO	SK	SL	ES	SV
													▲											
List of DGs and departments of the EC	BG	HR	CS	DA	NL	EN	ET	FI	FR	DE	EL	HU	IT	GA	LV	LT	MT	PL	PT	RO	SK	SL	ES	SV
																▲								
List of EU Commissioners	BG	HR		DA	NL	EN	ET		FR	DE	EL		IT	GA	LV	LT			PT	RO			ES	
				▲									▲			▲								
Council configurations	BG	HR		DA	NL		ET		FR	DE	EL		IT						PT	RO			ES	
													▲											
EP committees	BG	HR		DA	NL		ET		FR	DE	EL		IT						PT	RO			ES	
CoR – commissions	BG	HR		DA	NL					DE	EL		IT						PT	RO				
EESC – committees	BG			DA																				
				▲																				
European legislation																								
	▲						▲																	
EUR-Lex	BG	HR	CS	DA	NL	EN	ET	FI	FR	DE	EL	HU	IT	GA	LV	LT	MT	PL	PT	RO	SK	SL	ES	SV
	▲	▲	▲																					
PreLex / Legislative procedures	BG	HR	CS	DA	NL		ET																ES	
Official documents from EU institutions	BG						ET						IT											
CCVista		HR																		RO				
				▲			▲	▲					▲			▲				▲	▲			
EEA Agreement											EL										SK			SV

Table 2: A comparison of DGT webpages entitled "Guidelines for contractors translating into [LANGUAGE]", Section II. Contractor guides. Available from: https://ec.europa.eu/info/resources-partners/translation-and-drafting-resources/guidelines-translation-contractors_en (Accessed 2017-6-30)

Guidelines																								
																	▲							
Guide for contractors translating for the European Commission [Instructions for eXtra portal]	BG	HR	CS	DA	NL	EN	ET	FI	FR	DE	EL	HU	IT	GA	LV	LT	MT	PL	PT	RO	SK	SL	ES	SV
Translation checklist			CS	DA	NL	EN	ET	FI	FR	DE	EL	HU	IT	GA	LV	LT	MT		PT	RO	SK	SL	ES	SV
																				▲				
Translation Quality Info Sheets for Contractors		HR				EN							IT			LT	MT	PL		RO	SK			
Guidelines for translating into [LANGUAGE]					NL					DE							MT		PT	RO	SK			
			▲	▲								▲											▲	▲
Guidelines for translating and revising texts intended for the web		HR																						SV
										▲						▲	▲			▲				▲
EU terminology																								
IATE – EU terminology database	BG	HR	CS	DA	NL	EN	ET	FI	FR	DE	EL	HU	IT	GA	LV	LT	MT	PL	PT	RO	SK	SL	ES	SV
TARIC codes – online customs tariff database	BG	HR	CS	DA	NL	EN	ET	FI	FR	DE	EL	HU	IT	GA	LV	LT	MT	PL	PT	RO	SK	SL	ES	SV
EU Budget online	BG	HR	CS	DA	NL	EN	ET		FR	DE	EL	HU	IT		LV	LT	MT		PT	RO	SK	SL	ES	
Eurovoc – multilingual thesaurus covering EU policy fields	BG	HR	CS				ET		FR	DE		HU	IT		LV	LT			PT	RO	SK			
RAMON – Eurostat's statistical metadata website (including combined nomenclature)		HR	CS	DA	NL	EN	ET		FR	DE	EL	HU	IT		LV	LT	MT		PT	RO	SK		ES	SV
						▲										▲								

continued from preceding page

	Style guides																						
[LANGUAGE] style guide – DG Translation in-house styleguide	BG	HR		DA ▲		EN	ET	FI ▲		DE ▲	EL			GA ▲				PL ▲	PT	RO	SK	SL	ES	SV
Interinstitutional Style Guide – for [LANGUAGE]	BG	HR ▲	CS	DA	NL	EN ▲	ET	FI	FR	DE ▲	EL	HU	IT	GA ▲	LV	LT	MT	PL ▲	PT ▲	RO	SK	SL	ES ▲	SV ▲
Joint practical guide for persons involved in the drafting of EU legislation – for [LANGUAGE]	BG	HR	CS	DA	NL	EN ▲	ET	FI	FR	DE ▲	EL	HU	IT		LV	LT ▲	MT	PL	PT ▲	RO	SK	▲	ES ▲	SV
Joint Handbook for the Presentation and Drafting of Acts subject to the Ordinary Legislative Procedure		HR						FI								LT								
How to write clearly	▲					EN ▲	▲	▲		[DE]			IT		▲		MT							

Table 3: A comparison of DGT webpages entitled "Guidelines for contractors translating into [LANGUAGE]", Section III. Language-specific information.

Terminology and glossaries	BG	HR	CS	DA	EN	ET	FI	FR		EL	HU	IT	GA	LV	LT	MT		PT	RO	SK	SL	ES	SV
EU glossaries – on EUROPA (the EU's website)				DA	EN							IT						PT					SV
	▲	▲	▲	▲	▲	▲	▲	▲		▲	▲	▲	▲	▲	▲	▲		▲	▲	▲	▲	▲	▲
Models and templates	BG	HR	CS	DA	EN	ET	FI	FR	DE	EL	HU	IT		LV	LT	MT	PL	PT	RO		SL	ES	SV
LegisWrite models		HR	CS			ET				EL	HU			LV	LT		PL	PT	RO				
	▲	▲	▲	▲	▲	▲	▲	▲	▲	▲	▲	▲		▲	▲	▲	▲	▲	▲		▲	▲	▲
Useful links (national legislation / authorities / expert bodies)	BG		CS	DA	EN	ET		FR			HU	IT		LV				PT	RO		SL	ES	
N-Lex – national legislation databases of EU countries				DA	EN			FR										PT					
	▲		▲	▲		▲		▲			▲	▲		▲					▲		▲	▲	
Language magazine												IT				MT		PT				ES	
Language network												IT			LT					SK			

4.3.2 Overview and analysis of the content of the Resource webpages

Section I ("General EU information")

The first subsection entitled "EU institutions" of Section I (cf. Table 1) comprises of a total of 7 groups of resources. The first two ("Names of institutions, bodies and agencies of the EU" and "List of DGs and departments of the EC") are represented with each of the 24 webpages. The other five groups ("List of EU Commissioners", "Council configurations", "EP committees", "CoR – commissions", and "EESC – committees") are represented in 16, 12, 12, 9, and 2 cases, respectively. Two webpages stand out here, i.e. BG and DA, since they show all 7 resources.[16]

The second major subsection within Section I is called "European legislation" and it offers 6 categories. The picture suggested by the numbers is a mixed one as was the one above, too: Whereas the first category ("EUR-Lex") can be located in each of the 24 webpages, there are the remaining 4 categories ("PreLex / Legislative procedures", "Official documents from EU institutions", "CCVista", and "EEA Agreement") that are represented in the following way: 7, 3, 2 and 5, respectively.

Section II ("Contractor guides")

The first subsection ("Guidelines") has one category that is represented 100% across all the language-specific webpages, i.e. "Guide for contractors translating for the European Commission" (however, it needs to be considered in conjunction with "Instructions for eXtra portal", which is just another description for one and the same category. With the second category "Translation checklist", just three representations are missing, which shows that uniformity has not been achieved fully here. The remaining three ("Translation Quality Info Sheets for Contractors", "Guidelines for translating into [LANGUAGE]", and "Guidelines for translating and revising texts intended for the web") are represented in occurrences ranging from two to nine.

Under the second major subsection, "EU terminology", there are five categories: "IATE – EU terminology database"; "TARIC codes – online customs tariff database"; "EU Budget online"; "Eurovoc – multilingual thesaurus covering EU policy fields" and "RAMON – Eurostat's statistical metadata website (including

[16] The majority of departments (8) features just 2 pieces of resources; however, another high number of departments (7) offer 6 resources in this section.

combined nomenclature)". Whereas the first two are represented 100% across the language versions, the third (EU Budget online) sees 20 occurrences and the last of these (RAMON) occurs 19 times. The least represented category here is Eurovoc with roughly a little more than half of Resource pages mentioning it (i.e. 13 cases).

When it comes to the last subsection (Style guides) in Section II, only one category is mentioned in all 24 Resource pages: "Interinstitutional Style Guide – for [LANGUAGE]". The category "Joint practical guide for persons involved in the drafting of EU legislation – for [LANGUAGE]" is heavily represented with only two languages missing (GA, SL). The other three categories ("[LANGUAGE] style guide – DG Translation in-house styleguide", "Joint Handbook for the Presentation and Drafting of Acts subject to the Ordinary Legislative Procedure", and "How to write clearly") are represented in numbers ranging from more than half of the cases to just a few inclusions (16, 3 and 4 respectively).

Section III ("Language-specific information")

This section shows the lowest degree of uniformity. Not even the three major subsections – "Terminology and glossaries", "Models and templates", and "Useful links (national legislation / authorities / expert bodies)" are represented in all the language specific webpages. Thus, we find that the NL page lacks Section III altogether (among the 24 pages, it is the only one to leave a whole section out). While the subsection "Terminology and glossaries" is missing from the NL, DE, and PL pages, the subsection of "Models and templates" is missing from the NL, GA, and SK pages. The "Useful links" subsection is represented with just over half of the pages (13). The categories typically shown in this section tend to be represented in rather small numbers: 5, 10, 4, 4, and 3, respectively.[17]

4.3.3 Analysis of the content of individual pages

It should be borne in mind that all content analysis was carried out on the basis of the surface representation of links and/or link descriptions and not in an in-depth analysis of the individual sources. This limitation is intentional as an in-depth content analysis would not be practicable under the present research study design.

[17] That is, "EU glossaries – on EUROPA (the EU's website)"; "LegisWrite models"; "N-Lex – national legislation databases of EU countries"; "Language magazine"; "Language network".

In terms of quantity, the three subsections with the highest number of categories **represented across all 24 language Resource pages** (i.e. the most **harmonized subsections**) are the following: "EU institutions", "European legislation", and "Guidelines" (with 7, 6, and 6 categories, respectively). The categories that are represented in 100% of the cases are the following:

- Names of institutions, bodies and agencies of the EU,
- List of DGs and departments of the EC,
- EUR-Lex,
- IATE, EU terminology database,
- TARIC codes, online customs tariff database,
- Interinstitutional Style Guide for [LANGUAGE],
- Guide for contractors translating for the European Commission [Instructions for eXtra portal].

The order of information as presented within subsections varies, yet not to a very significant degree. For example, while most of the Resource pages feature the category of "LegisWrite models" (i.e. templates for the layout of specific EU legislative documents) first in the list under the subsection "Models and templates" within Section III (this is true for 6 of the 10 pages that feature this source), we find it in the 7th, 4th, 6th, and 2nd position among the sources listed on the Czech, Latvian, Lithuanian, and Polish webpages. Obviously, this **lack of complete cross-language alignment** is rather insignificant, especially as it still occurs within one and the same subsection across language versions. There are, however, cases of resources featured in locations varying in terms of whole sections, such as a resource on clear writing ("How to write clearly"). Whereas EN, IT and MT pages place it in Section II (in subsection "Style guides".[18]), the Finnish page has it in Section III (subsection "Models and templates")

Apart from the resources mentioned in the categories (i.e. those that occur twice or more times across the language versions), there is a considerable wealth of **unique information**, being largely language and/or country specific. The proportion of this unique information is huge, amounting to almost exactly 50% of the entire pool of the resources.[19] Most of the unique links can be found in the Swedish and Lithuanian (50+ each) language pages, and the Romanian, Italian,

[18]The German page features it in the same Section II, yet under subsection Guidelines.

[19]In fact, 395 unique sources were counted, which is 49.8% of the total of 793.

Bulgarian and Czech pages show more than twenty resources each. Less than 10 unique resources can be found on the Dutch, Hungarian, Greek, Polish, Portuguese, French, Finnish, English and Slovak pages (listed in ascending order in terms of the number of occurrences). The remaining 9 pages have between 10 and 19 unique sources. The circumstance that the French and English language departments do not deem it necessary to upload specific (unique) material in large volumes may be due to the fact that these are procedural languages and serve as source languages comparably more often than the other languages.

4.4 Analysis of links

The following is a detailed analysis of the links[20] as featured on the individual 24 webpages of the DGT Resources page. The analysis of the wealth of data available was carried out on two levels. First, all the links were taken together and examined in terms of link address, and, second, the link face text (which users normally see as the colored and underlined text) was analyzed, including some approximations on the actual content of the resources referred to. While the findings are presented in this section, they are discussed in §5.

4.4.1 Analysis of link addresses and their provenance

Altogether, the DGT Resource website contains 24 webpages, including a total of 793 hyperlinks[21], i.e. interactive fields representing individual references. The number of resources contained on individual (language specific) webpages totals from 71 (Lithuanian) to 17 (Dutch and Polish).

As for first-level domains, the *.eu* domain has 401 occurrences (i.e. 51%), other top-level domains represented in the linked sites/files include the following:[22]

[20]To give a few examples of the link texts – and for the sake of interest – here are the two longest links of all those featured in the research corpus: eur-lex.europa.eu/search.html?or0=DN%3D32012r0966*,DN-old%3D32012r0966*&qid=1467623088973&DTS_DOM=EU_LAW&type=advanced&lang=en&SUBDOM_INIT=LEGISLATION&DTS_SUBDOM=LEGISLATION ec.europa.eu/info/resources-partners/translation-and-drafting-resources/guidelines-translation-contractors/guidelines-contractors-translating-romanian_de. On the contrary, the shortest links read csic.es, uni.com, ritap.es, kotus.fi, and legex.ro. A typical link looks like this: http://ec.europa.eu/info/files/czech-resources-combined-nomenclature-en-cs-tmx_cs.

[21]On average, there are 33 resources per Resource webpage.

[22]Interestingly, there are EU first-level domains that refer to an EU country where an EU official language is spoken, yet are not represented in the list above (such as .cz/, .mt/, .pl/, .pt/, .si/, .sk/), which means that the Czech, Maltese, Polish, Portuguese, Slovenian and Slovak language resource pages do not link to resources hosted on the respective national domain at all. This is explained by the fact that although there is language-specific content given on the Resource webpages, it may be placed on the europa.eu server, not linked directly to the country resource.

- `.it` (15 occurrences),
- `.ie` (13 occurrences),
- `.lt` (10 occurrences),
- `.ro` (8 occurrences),
- `.com`, `.es`, `.fi`, `.hr`, `.org` (6 occurrences each),
- `.lv`, `.se` (4 occurrences each),
- `.be` (3 occurrences),
- `.bg`, `.ch`, `.dk`, `.ee`, `.hu`, `.nl`, `.si` (2 occurrences each),
- `.de`, `.edu`, `.fr`, `.int`, `.lu`, `.ru`, `.uk` (1 occurrence each).

As regards second-level domains, the *europa.eu* domain (EU official website domain) is represented by 396 occurrences, which means that only five of the 401 .eu hyperlinks link to websites other than the europa.eu website. Third-level domains include predominantly the EU Commission domain with the domain name "ec.europa.eu" occurring 136 times (17% of all the links in the research corpus). Of this pool, there seem to be only five cases of a direct link to the DGT website (featuring the "ec.europa.eu/translation/" path). Other EC's DGs and services referred to, according to the link address, include DG Agriculture and Rural Development, DG Budget, Eurostat, DG Health and Food Safety, Joint Research Centre, DG Justice and Consumers, and DG Taxation and Customs Union.

To make the above information complete, the proportion of linked sites vs. linked files in the resources pool was also surveyed. The expressions `file/files/.pdf/.zip` occur in 362 links (whether once or multiple times), which also indicates the number of files linked on the Resource website.

4.4.2 Approximation of the content based on the hyperlink surface text

When it comes to the most frequently occurring link tags, i.e. the hyperlink face text, which appears as the title of the hyperlink, "Interinstitutional Style Guide" (EU institutions' main SG), "EUR-Lex" (the EU's legislation repository), and "IATE" (EU termbank) appear 25 times each. Additionally, "List of directorates-general and departments of the European Commission" as well as "Names of institutions, bodies and agencies of the European Union" and "TARIC codes" have 24 occurrences each; further, "Joint practical guide for persons involved in the drafting of EU legislation" and "Translation checklist" occur 19 times. These link tags give a tentative indication of what topics are most frequently represented in the resources pool, thus pointing to the importance that the website owner has attributed to them.

4.4.2.1 Explicit referrals to quality aspects

In order to see to what extent the goal of the SGs and translation manuals (which, ultimately, is maintaining/raising product quality) is mentioned explicitly in the caption texts, the following expressions were searched: qualit*, term*, glossar*, corp*, harmonis*, standard*, require* and others (see below). They stand for topics linked with ensuring standardization and harmonization (e.g., by managing terminology, glossaries, corpora), with introducing requirements and with providing further search and information sources.

4.4.2.2 The expression of quality *per se*

The expression "qualit*"[23] is encountered 9 times altogether in the research corpus, i.e. in three types of resources. The surface titles of the links are as follows: DG Translation Quality Guidelines, Quality criteria for translating into German, Translation Quality Info Sheet, and Translation quality info sheets for contractors (the last one occurs 6 times).

4.4.2.3 Guidelines, manuals, requirements

The expression "guide*" is represented 109 times altogether. The type of resource most commonly referred to is a "guide" (89 occurrences), followed by "guidelines" (18 occurrences). According to the DGT resources pages, guides/guidelines can be "brief", "specific", or "essential". They differ according to their focus (Spelling guide, Editing guidelines for translators, Guide to eurojargon, Guide to writing clear administrative Italian, Guidelines on terminology) or scope (Interinstitutional Style Guide, Interinstitutional Style Guide – for Czech, Interinstitutional Style Guide – for French..., Joint practical guide for persons involved in the drafting of EU legislation – for Bulgarian, Joint practical guide for persons involved in the drafting of EU legislation – for German...). They may be text type specific: Guidelines for translating and revising Commission communications; or they may be for detailing the purpose of translations: Guidelines for translating

[23]The asterisk designates a truncated string of characters. This means that when searching for „qualit*", expressions such as quality, qualities, qualitative, qualitatively, etc. can be found.

and revising texts intended for the general public, Guidelines for translating and revising texts intended for the web.

Most of the language departments have their own style guides: English Style Guide, Finnish style guide, German translation style guide, Greek style guide, etc. Guides can differ according to the target group: "Guide for contractors translating for the European Commission", "The Joint Handbook for the presentation and drafting of acts subject to the ordinary legislative procedure", "Polish in-house style guide" (which is primarily, yet not exclusively intended for EC in-house staff), "DG Translation in-house handbook for Danish (Visdomsbogen)". They can also be rather general: "DG Translation Quality Guidelines", "Linguistic guidelines for translators". There can even be "meta"-style guides: "Using style guides – in what order?" (on the German Resource page) or "Integrated system of Lithuanian language resources".

The expression "manual" is used in a rather limited way: There are only five occurrences of this term: "Legislative drafting manual", "Manual of precedents for acts established within the Council of the European Union" (under two language pages), "Manual of Precedents for International Agreements and Related Acts" and "Revision manual".

As regards other expressions used to denote the nature of the resource, there are some that suggest the binding nature of a document, such as: "decree for transliteration", "rules", "translation conventions", "terms and linguistic norms", "normative translation memory". Besides, there is also a number of guide types, the binding nature of which is weaker: "Consolidated linguistic advice", "Czech orthography recommendation", "Tips for better language". While "requirements" is featured just once ("Basic requirements for terms"), "instructions" tends to be rather frequent ("Instructions for eXtra portal", "Instructions for translating", "Instructions on the use of xliff files", "Maltese Freelance Instructions", "Specific instructions for different document types", etc.).

Finally, there are models ("Explanatory memorandum model", "Legal Service models", "Legislative financial statement model", "LegisWrite models and translation memories"), templates ("Thematic templates and translation memories"), checklists ("Checklist for outgoing translations", "Pre-delivery checklist") and quite a lot of the guides are entitled using a *How to* question: "How to refer to EFSA documents", "How to search EU case law", "How to use IATE?", "How to write clearly (4x)", etc. Altogether, there are well over 130 sources presented as types of guides/guidelines/manuals as listed in this subsection.

4.4.2.4 Harmonization/standardization

The usage of the above expressions varies: "harmonis*" occurs just twice and seems to denote two different realities, one evoking the legislative process ("Harmonisation of Hungarian law with EU legislation") and the other referring to consistency requirements ("Harmonised geographical names"). The expression "standard" can be found eight times in the following resource titles and, equally, pointing to a varied understanding of the expression, from official standards/ norms to consistency issues: "Lithuanian standards board term base", "National Organisation for Standardization", "Register of standardised terms", "Revised official Irish language standard", "Standard clauses for explanatory memorandum", "Standard ending of the notice (LT-EN-FR-DE)", "Standard forms for public procurement", "UN/ECE standard phrases". The expression "common" denotes the following references: "Common phrases (EN-LT)", "Common titles of German legislative acts", and others.

4.4.2.5 Terminology rules

The expression "term*" (standing for terminology, terms, etc.) appears 40 times.[24] There are 33 mentions of "glossar*" in the research corpus.[25] Electronic corpora are referred to eight times in total.[26] Other relevant terms in this regard involve

[24]Here are a few examples: *Agreed terminology, solved linguistic issues and slogans; Application for recognition of a traditional term; Basic requirements for terms; Budget terminology; English-Lithuanian dictionary of polytechnics terms; European Parliament glossary database TermCoord; Finnish Centre for Technical Terminology; Fishery terms; Glossary of energy terms; Irish terminology handbook; Language and terminology newsletter; Lithuanian standards board term base; Non-Iate Termbase; Procurement terminology; Schengen and migration terminology; Slovak Terminology Network (STS); State aid terminology; Statistics terms; terminography; The National Terminology Database for Irish; Theory of terminology.*

[25]Here are selected examples: *Anti-dumping glossary; Asylum and migration glossary; Civil and commercial law glossary; Council glossaries; Customs glossary; Environment glossary; EU budget glossary; Glossary in the field of concurrence; Glossary of administrative language; Glossary of languages and countries; Glossary of primary law; Glossary of security documents, security features and other related technical terms; Nuclear energy glossary; Phytosanitary glossary; Railway glossary.*

[26]These include: "Croatian Language Corpus", "Croatian National Corpus" (HR), "Aligned corpus of English to Irish translations", "Aligned corpus of English to Irish translations – legislative texts", "The New Corpus for Ireland – corpus of Irish language texts" (GA), "Lithuanian language corpus", "Corpus of Academic Lithuanian" and "Corpus of computer lexis and phrases" (LT).

"vocabulary",[27] "expressions",[28] "dictionary,"[29] or "database".[30] Taken together, these terminology-related expressions appear 104 times.

4.4.2.6 Information sites and further references

Resources include not only manuals and templates to abide by when translating. Many other documents/references of an informative nature can be found in the featured resources as well: "Dumping explained", "Misused English words and expressions in EU publications", "The evaluation of Freelance Document", "Translating from Slovak into English", "Translating online content", "Translation patterns", "Translation problems and difficulties", "Translation quality info sheets for contractors", "Typical translation mistakes". Designations like "Language and translation reference site" or "Legislative portal" are used to refer to other resources that are either a hub, a collection of further resources, and/or a repository.

5 Discussion of results

5.1 Overall findings related to SGs/TMs

5.1.1 Recipients

Although called "Guidelines for translation contractors", the resources are used by internal staff, too. Not only that, some of the materials are even labelled "in-house" (style guides), which would suggest that they had been created for the principal use of internal staff.

5.1.2 Structure and statistics

As mentioned above, there are 793 hyperlinks/references to all the 24 DGT Resource webpages. Interpreting the quantitative results,[31] we see a rather misbalanced picture: The webpage with the highest number of resources (Lithuanian) features almost five times more items than the pages of the least resources available (Dutch and Polish), thus accounting for almost 10% of all the resources from

[27] Cf. "Antidumping vocabulary", "EU common procurement vocabulary", "Gender equality vocabulary".

[28] Cf. "Austrian expressions".

[29] Cf. "English-Bulgarian polytechnic dictionary".

[30] Cf. "Danish legal database", "Finnish grammar database", "Irish placenames database".

[31] Cf. §4.2 Quantitative overview of the resources.

the resource pool. The lack of linked materials with NL and PL can be explained either by the fact that the sites are still under construction due to the recent overhaul of the Europa website or, otherwise, by a lack of resources, thus there being a low priority attributed to the issue of SGs/TMs. The cases of RO and BL ranking 3rd and 5th respectively might be due to the fact that the countries joined the EU quite recently and had a wealth of sources available at entry, which they later complemented with their own materials. Another stimulus for an increased production and representation of SGs/TMs might also be a poor experience with contractors. However, should the attempt be undertaken to explain the disparity between language departments by hinting to the year of accession to the EU alone and a degree of possible resource saturation resulting from it, this would be easily proven wrong: there can hardly be a better example than the 30–40 band with the Estonian, Danish, Czech, Croatian, Spanish, and German ones: Although each country joined the EU in a different year (2004, 1973, 2004, 2013, 1986, 1957, respectively, with, obviously, Germany being among the founding member states), they still offer a very similar number of resources.

Other possible explanations come to mind,[32] one of which is the idiosyncratic factor (i.e. outside the scope of the top-down coordination/harmonization effort), and another is the different approaches to collecting/presenting the material (e.g., the German in-house style guide is long and incorporates some information which, on other language departments' webpages, is scattered across several documents).

Ten out of the 24 Resource webpages come together in the 20–30 tier, and the share of this band within the entire resource pool accounts for a third of the resources (32%). This suggests that should there be a further requirement for page layout uniformity and resource availability, a common structure of the pages could involve 11 common resources featured more or less across the board, complemented by some 10+ language department-specific resources.

5.1.3 Content

As regards the content of individual pages, it was found that the distinction between the pages which have **all three subheadings and those that have less or none**, does not follow a pattern – neither according to the year of accession (e.g., 2004, when 10 new member states joined the EU), nor according to the status of the language represented (e.g., procedural vs. non-procedural languages). Thus,

[32]For the following hints, I owe my appreciation to Łucja Biel's comments. Other suggestions are included in §6, Limitations of the study and outlook for further research.

the fact that some subsections are missing in one page and are present in another may simply be linked with the (un)availability of specific resources for specific languages. This, in turn, is due to language policy and other demand generating aspects, such as cooperation with contractors, the perceived need on the part of members of the service, etc. Another, and quite practical reason might be differences in human resources available to maintain the webpage.

The analysis of **the most harmonized sections** shows that Section II (Contractor guides) includes three subsections and three categories, which are identical across the resource pool. Section I (General EU information) shows two shared subsections and three categories represented across the board. This proves a harmonized approach in a number of areas, in a top-down attitude. The **seven categories that are represented 100%** across all the language specific Resource pages signify the importance attributed to them by decision-makers; the categories include references to EU institutions and DGT departments, terminology resources and the Interinstitutional Style Guide (IISG). It comes as no surprise that it is Section III (Language-specific information) that shows the greatest variation – i.e. the least harmonization with only 5 categories, none of which is represented fully across the language-specific pages.

The study has also shown that in terms of **cross-language alignment** (i.e. similar sources featured at similar locations across language-specific pages), the structure of individual Resource pages is almost always kept homogenous. Although, admittedly, there are exceptions (sources shown at other locations within the page structure when comparing language versions), they do not pose a major challenge for the user, as hardly any user (apart from researchers) would be looking for resources across a great many of individual pages.

At first glance (taken together), the Resource website shows a strikingly even representation of **non-unique sources** (those featured at least twice across the board) and **unique sources**, at a ratio of 1:1. However, a closer analysis of individual pages reveals that the majority show between 10 and 19 unique sources (9 pages out of the 24) while, for example, the Swedish and Lithuanian pages top the list with 50+ such links each. This shows yet another aspect of **variation** among the Resource pages.

The **link text analysis** shows that the resources are largely Europe bound; in the majority of cases (50%), they refer to the EU official site (europa.eu). As regards the percentage of linked files vs. site links, almost half (46%) of the links refer to files, whereas the rest refer to other websites (where subsequent links are likely to be found).

When the **content was extrapolated based on the hyperlink text**, it was observed that where there are frequent occurrences of a text sequence, it reflects the standard structure of the individual pages. As regards the description of individual sources and their (tentative) binding nature, they are listed under varying labels. The list ranges from tips, *How to* manuals, advice, recommendations, and checklists to templates/models, guidelines, requirements, instructions, rules, conventions, norms, and even a "decree". The most frequently used expression to denote the nature of a resource is as a "guide".

Terminology sources are listed under highly varying labels, too, which, arguably, are used as synonyms quite often. Quantitatively, the most frequently represented sources are guides/guidelines, followed by terminology resources and information sites and further references.

5.2 Findings related to quality

Translation quality is explicitly mentioned only once on the DGT's homepage under "Clear writing – translation quality". This does not mean that quality was of little concern to the service:[33] users only need to proceed further to tap into the information available.

It has been shown (see above) that major areas of interest when it comes to translation product quality (information/reference sources, harmonization of terminology and style guides) are covered substantially in the Resources website. Somewhat surprisingly, though, the analysis of explicit referrals to the quality aspects among the collection of resources shows that the expression "quality" occurs only 9 times overall, which accounts for one percent of all the links referred to. Moreover, these nine occurrences include only three types of linked resources as one of the three resource types is present across 7 language versions.

5.3 Similarity and difference to the survey of 2013

With the overhaul of the EU's web, the concept of lean pages has been introduced, which is the rule of thumb today, and it is useful when accessing the site from a mobile device. However, much detailed information had to be sacrificed to this leanness as the comparison with a previous study on SGs/TMs shows (cf. Svoboda 2013). As regards organization and presentation of the material, the DGT resources still show a significant variation in terms of both the extent and the topics of material represented – this is an observation, not a judgement.

[33]In fact the opposite is true, cf. the publications section.

What is striking is the current lack of multilingual information presented on the pages. The Resources web is now fully Anglophone; even the pages concerning language-specific issues are presented in English only.[34] Previously, there was an option to switch between at least two languages (typically English and the language of the Resource page concerned, e.g., English and Czech). The present state is a paradox given the EU's proclaimed commitment to multilingualism and the DG's merit (serving the multilingualism policy). Moreover, the pages are typically entitled "Guidelines for contractors translating into [language]" and serve users translating not only from English, thus there might be a considerable language barrier for users with little or no command of English. However, for the purposes of this research, the current extensive survey would have been impossible if the pages had remained localized in the source languages. The reason is that much information used to be incomparable on the old web as not all items were translated and the endeavor to have all the language specific references translated into one language of comparison first would prove impracticable under the present study design. What has improved substantially, though, is the user experience when navigating through the pages and a relatively easy-to-conceive structure of the pages.

5.4 Considerations as regards the initial assumptions

In §3, Methodology, four assumptions have been presented, given the fact that they concern the main area of interest here, i.e. SGs/TMs as quality assurance indicators. Here, they will be re-iterated and compared to the research findings. The **first assumption**, i.e. that institutional translation is a field characterized by standardization, is confirmed for DGT, when taken to mean a top-down approach, and when limiting it to the aspect of SGs/TMs. This is true for a number of reasons: (i) The existence of a resource site, especially in an institution, such as DGT, with multiple language departments, bears witness to a concerted (managerial) standardization effort. (ii) DGT shows a trend of standardizing even the guiding/standardization sources (compared to 2013, the number of sources has

[34]There are just a handful of resources that are entitled in a language other than English, e.g., "Brocardi e latinismi", "Gemeinsames Handbuch", "Gwida Prattika Komuni", "Moniteur belge", "Rete per l'eccellenza dell'italiano istituzionale". On the other hand, some resources are available in two or more languages indeed, yet the respective page is still in English only. What is also user unfriendly, to a certain degree, is the fact that there is neither a link to the DGT homepage, nor the possibility to go to the resources page once the user has landed on a page offering the download of a specific resource document (e.g., when following a direct link, the Go Back function is then not available).

been reduced – an entire section has been discarded – and the overall structure of the Resource website has been harmonized – now, the webpages are featured in English only). The **second assumption**, i.e. that the amount and the nature of references used as part of the translator resources will vary among Resource pages, was verified, given the fact that 50% of resources are of a unique nature (cf. §5.1 above), thus there exists a certain (albeit limited) degree of variation as regards cross-language alignment of the sources and there is considerable variation when referring to a certain type of resource (cf. the numerous types of guides/guidelines and terminology resources). **The third assumption** (the resource material will relate to reference materials, terminology, style/style guides) has been verified for DGT in full (cf. §5.1 with the following areas that are 100% harmonized across language versions: references to EU institutions and DGT departments, terminology resources and the IISG).[35] **The fourth assumption** (the quality aspect of institutional translation is governed by rules) could be verified only indirectly for DGT, using the given research corpus. On the face of it, the Resource website features very many guides and instructions (i.e. rules) concerning a large array of topics, yet these rules are explicitly linked to quality in only 1% of the resource titles (cf. §5.2). This would suggest that there is no direct link between rules and the quality requirement. On the other hand, abandoning the explicit side of things and involving quality related features (such as harmonization of terminology and style, using recommended technology and information sources, etc.) into a broader aspect of quality assurance procedures, the link between the wealth of the DGT resource (i.e. rules which deal with exactly the above instances and aspects) and the quality aspect becomes obvious.

6 Limitations of the study and implications for further research

The limitations include data collection and data processing accuracy, since, to a considerable extent, these processes took place manually and the resource pool was rather extensive. Any content analysis presented here was carried out on the basis of the surface representation of links and/or link descriptions, not based on any in-depth analysis of the individual sources (this means that, under the present research study design, hardly any of the almost 800 source pages of this world's largest translation resource were actually accessed and consulted

[35]The analysis of harmonized sections suggests that they had been identified in a managerial approach, which, at the same time, reflects the fact that the sources were considered mission-critical for the institution.

in terms of their actual content). Further investigation is needed into the responsibility structures for maintaining the resource pages; valuable information for the explanatory part would certainly be gained from interviewing the stakeholders. Likewise, it was outside the scope of this study to actually trace the implementation of the SGs/TMs in translation products and their impact on actual translation product quality. Prospects for further research include corpus analysis based on the surface texts shown in individual webpages, in order to identify recurring keywords and further textual arrangements. In future studies, more detailed analyses of the individual materials will be necessary as well as conducting similar surveys of a general nature on translation departments of other institutions (EU and other) to show similarities, patterns, and differences and to point to specific and recurring phenomena, which will place the present data in a broader perspective.

7 Conclusion

The intention of the present chapter was to present quantitative data on the number and extent of the resources available especially to DGT contractors, to categorize the material and to find significant representations in terms of the content and its implicit or explicit reference to the quality aspect. It has been observed that the Resource webpages are largely structured in a uniform way. They testify to the effort invested by the DGT service into the standardization and harmonization of its translation process and products and, as a consequence, its goal to maintain and support process and product quality. On the other hand, despite this clearly documented goal, the DGT resources still show a significant variation in terms of both the extent and the topics of material represented. Nevertheless, the wealth and level of detail of the TMs and SGs represented in the DGT Resources website illustrate some of the challenges of the so-called institutional EU translation as a service: for their translations to be considered high quality, the translators (both contractors and in-house translators) have to follow very many recommendations and instructions.

Translation manuals have accompanied major translation projects in the history of translating (cf. Kang 2009: 142 and other research). First and foremost, they represent the prescriptive approach to regulating translator choices. As such, they are key to translation practice and, in effect, to Translation Studies researches, who study such practice. This is particularly true for the field of institutional translation. Translation Studies scholars should pay attention to TMs/SGs for a number of reasons. From the diachronic point of view, they are an invaluable account of a translation team's deliberations and choices over time as their shared "institutional" memory. From the synchronic viewpoint, they offer a backdrop for evaluation of existing translation products within communication processes where TMs/SGs are to be observed. If it is true that TMs/SGs are constitutive to the notion of translation quality and, in effect, to institutional translation in the supranational/international contexts (cf. §2 above), they need to be understood in more detail. Consequently, further studies into this area are needed to understand better and compare the practices at other institutions and in other settings. Such understanding will, in turn, contribute to singling out the specifics of the translation process/products in the field of institutional translation, and help distinguish this particular field within the discipline of Translation Studies at large.

References

Becker-Mrotzek, Michael. 1990. Kommunikation und Sprache in Institutionen. Ein Forschungsbericht zur Analyse institutioneller Kommunikation. Teil I: Sammelbände mit Arbeiten zur Kommunikation in Instituionen und Monographien zu Beratungen in Institutionen. *Deutsche Sprache* 2. 158–190.

Biel, Łucja. 2017. Quality in institutional EU translation: Parameters, policies and practices. In Tomáš Svoboda, Łucja Biel & Krzysztof Łoboda (eds.), *Quality aspects in institutional translation* (Translation and Multilingual Natural Language Processing 8), 31–57. Berlin: Language Science Press. DOI:10.5281/zenodo.1048183

Directorate-General for Translation (DGT), European Commission. 2008. *Guide for external translators.* http://ec.europa.eu/translation/documents/guide_contractors_en.pdf, accessed 2012-5-28.

Directorate-General for Translation (DGT), European Commission. 2012. *Quantifying quality costs and the cost of poor quality in translation. quality efforts and the consequences of poor quality in the European Commission's Directorate-General for Translation.* Luxembourg: Publications Office of the European Union.

Directorate-General for Translation (DGT), European Commission. 2013. *Document quality control in public administrations and international organisations.* Luxembourg.

Drugan, Joanna, Ingemar Strandvik & Erkka Vuorinen. 2018. Translation quality, quality management and agency: principles and practice in the European Union institutions. In Joss Moorkens, Sheila Castilho, Stephen Doherty & Federico Gaspari (eds.), *Translation quality assessment: from principles to practice.* Berlin: Springer.

Felipe Boto, Maria del Rosario & Martín José Fernández Antolín. 2009. *La traducción de textos normativos en el ámbito institucional de la Unión Europea [The translation of normative texts in the institutional field of the European Union].* http://unilat.org/Library/Handlers/File.ashx?id=5154ac8d-935d-4611-9c93-de7fb898ff09, accessed 2017-9-29.

Halverson, Sandra L. 2008. Translations as institutional facts: An ontology for assumed translation. In Anthony Pym, Miriam Shlesinger & Daniel Simeoni (eds.), *Beyond descriptive translation studies. Investigations in homage to Gideon Toury*, 343–362. Amsterdam: John Benjamins.

Kang, Ji-Hae. 2009. Institutional translation. In Mona Baker & Gabriela Saldanha (eds.), *Routledge encyclopaedia of translation studies*, 141–144. London & New York: Routledge.

Koskinen, Kaisa. 2008. *Translating institutions. an ethnographic study of EU translation.* Manchester: St. Jerome.

Koskinen, Kaisa. 2011. Institutional translation. In Yves Gambier & Luc van Doorslaer (eds.), *Handbook of translation studies*, vol. 2, 54–60. Amsterdam: John Benjamins.

Mason, Ian. 2004 [2003]. Text parameters in translation: transitivity and institutional cultures. In Lawrence Venuti (ed.), *The Translation Studies reader*, 2nd edn., 470–481. New York/London: Routledge.

Prieto Ramos, Fernando (ed.). 2017. *Institutional translation for international governance: enhancing quality in multilingual legal communication.* London: Bloomsbury.

Schäffner, Christina, Luciana Sabina Tcaciuc & Wine Tesseur. 2014. Translation practices in political institutions: a comparison of national, supranational, and non-governmental organisations. *Perspectives. Studies in Translatology* 22(4). 493–510. DOI:10.1080/0907676X.2014.948890

Sosoni, Vilelmini. 2011. Training translators to work for the EU institutions: luxury or necessity. *The Journal of Specialised Translation* 16. 77–108.

Strandvik, Ingemar. 2017a. Evaluation of outsourced translations. State of play in the European Commission's Directorate-General for Translation (DGT). In Tomáš Svoboda, Łucja Biel & Krzysztof Łoboda (eds.), *Quality aspects in institutional translation* (Translation and Multilingual Natural Language Processing 8), 123–137. Berlin: Language Science Press. DOI:10.5281/zenodo.1048194

Strandvik, Ingemar. 2017b. Towards a more structured approach to quality assurance: DGT's quality journey. In Fernando Prieto Ramos (ed.), *Institutional translation for international governance: enhancing quality in multilingual legal communication*, 51–62. London: Bloomsbury.

Svoboda, Tomáš. Forthcoming. Institutional translation in national contexts. Quality assurance in governmental institutions across Europe. In Éric Poirier & Daniel Gallego Hernández (eds.), *Current approaches to business and institutional translation*. Québec: Cambridge Scholars Publishing.

Svoboda, Tomáš. 2008. Ubi sunt homines? Poznámky k řízení kvality překladů u Generálního ředitelství pro překlad Evropské komise [Ubi sunt homines? On Translation Quality Management at the European Commission's Directorate-General for Translation]. In Alena Ďuricová (ed.), *Od textu k prekladu II*, 143–151. Prague: Jednota tlumočníků a překladatelů.

Svoboda, Tomáš. 2013. Translation manuals and drafting style guides at the European Commission. *Le Bulletin du CRATIL Centre de recherche de l'ISIT* 10. http://www.lebulletinducratil.fr/index.php/en/translation-manuals-and-drafting-style-guides-at-the-european-commission, accessed 2017-8-30.

Vandepitte, Sonia. 2017. Translation product quality: A conceptual analysis. In Tomáš Svoboda, Łucja Biel & Krzysztof Łoboda (eds.), *Quality aspects in institutional translation* (Translation and Multilingual Natural Language Processing 8), 15–29. Berlin: Language Science Press. DOI:10.5281/zenodo.1048180

Chapter 6

Terminology work in the European Commission: Ensuring high-quality translation in a multilingual environment

Karolina Stefaniak

Directorate-General for Translation, European Commission

Terminology is an integral part of every translation process, necessary to achieve high-quality translation. In the case of EU law, terminology is additionally a matter of legal certainty and clarity. Terminological errors may lead to citizens and companies misunderstanding their rights and obligations, make the harmonization of laws between Member States more difficult and often result in legal disputes at national or EU level, thus tarnishing the image of the European Union and its institutions. This is why EU language services place great emphasis on terminology work and on integrating terminology in their translation process. The aim of terminology work is, firstly, to give translators timely terminological support: to find a correct equivalent, to clear the meaning of a concept, to coin a brand new term or to help them choose the right equivalent in a given context, out of many equally correct terms, based on the criteria of consistency, accuracy and clarity. Secondly, the aim of terminology work is to manage the existing terminology resources. This work is both of a descriptive and prescriptive nature and the central hub for EU terminology is the multilingual termbase IATE, jointly managed by several EU institutions and accessible also to the general public. This chapter describes how the terminology work is done in the Directorate-General for Translation of the European Commission on the example of the practices in the Polish Language Department.

Karolina Stefaniak. 2017. Terminology work in the European Commission: Ensuring high-quality translation in a multilingual environment. In Tomáš Svoboda, Łucja Biel & Krzysztof Łoboda (eds.), *Quality aspects in institutional translation*, 109–121. Berlin: Language Science Press. DOI:10.5281/zenodo.1048192

1 Introduction

Almost every EU institution has its own translation service and almost all of these services also do terminology work,[1] alongside translation, organized both on the central level, in terminology coordination units, and on the local level, in language departments. Terminology coordination units cooperate with each other on the interinstitutional level and deal mostly with multilingual projects. Language departments, on the other hand, work on bilingual projects. Everybody involved in terminology work follows the same general good practices, however, actual terminology work may look slightly different in each institution and in each department, depending on the needs of the translation service in question and its resources.

Terminology work is carried out in tight connection with the texts being translated. On the one hand, it consists in solving ongoing terminology problems, which are lodged in by translators when they are working on a text. On the other hand, systematic terminology work is conducted, which consists in collecting and processing terms from the text to be translated, if possible, even before the translator starts working on it. The extraction of terms from the source text and the clarification of the concepts are usually done by the central terminology unit. When their part is ready, language departments start working on equivalents of extracted terms in their languages. Less often, terminology work consists of developing a conceptual system for a given domain; such projects usually aim at deleting duplicates from the termbases and consolidating the existing entries, and they are conducted in cooperation with other interested EU institutions.

The main source of terminology for all EU institutions is IATE[2] – InterActive Terminology for Europe – a multilingual terminology database launched in 2004. Before that EU terminology was created, collected, stored and managed separately by various institutions in a few collections and termbases. These resources were later imported to IATE. There are at present about 8.6 million terms in IATE, distributed through approximately 1.4 million entries, in 24 official EU languages (and in some other languages like Russian, Chinese, Arabic

[1]Terminology work is "work concerned with the systematic collection, description, processing and presentation of concepts and their designations". A concept is a "unit of knowledge created by a unique combination" of properties common to a set of objects. A designation is a "representation of a concept by a sign which denotes it"; designations can be symbols, appellations or terms (cf. ISO 1087-1:2000). Part of terminology work is terminology management, which is concerned with the recording and presentation of data.

[2]iate.europa.eu

and also Latin).[3] The database is concept-oriented, i.e. one entry corresponds to one concept. It is jointly administered by the European Commission, the European Parliament, the Council of the EU, the Court of Justice, the European Court of Auditors, the Committee of the Regions, the European Economic and Social Committee, the European Central Bank, the European Investment Bank and the Translation Centre for the Bodies of the European Union. IATE was made available to the public in 2007.

The main reason for the existence of IATE is to facilitate multilingual drafting and translating of EU legal texts. This is why the database contains not only terms in the narrow sense, but also quasi-terms, proper names, abbreviations, titles and phrases that repeatedly occur or could occur in EU texts and which should be uniformly used and translated. The amount of information entered in IATE should be sufficient for an unequivocal identification of the concept in question and should have added value in respect to information commonly available in other sources. Owing to the way IATE was created, the quality of the entries still varies substantially, from very well edited entries in all languages, to entries completed only by few language departments and containing very little information. Entries containing at least one term, a reliable source for that term and a definition are considered high-quality entries (when there is no definition, at least the context for the usage of the term should be given for the entry to be considered high-quality). Thus, terminology work also consists in constant monitoring of the use of terms and the subsequent updating, correcting or completing of the relevant IATE entries. Terms, like all other components of the specialized language, evolve, get accepted or rejected, change their conceptual scope, go out of usage or become marked. All these processes need to be properly registered.

2 Terminology work in the Directorate-General for Translation (DGT) of the European Commission

The aim of DGT it to supply the Commission services with high-quality translations, whereby quality is understood as the degree to which translation corresponds to the expressed or implied expectations of the recipients (cf. ISO 9000:2015). Terminology is considered to be a key element of translation, without which high quality cannot be achieved. The process of translation in DGT is a team effort with translation and terminological decisions often being taken collectively. The simplest scenario involves two translators – the first translat-

[3]Data from May 2016.

ing the text and the second revising it. However, if any of them has questions or doubts concerning terminology, he or she contacts the department terminologist, who assists them in finding answers to their questions and suggests solutions.

Requests from translators usually concern assistance in finding an equivalent for a challenging term or in coining a new term. The terminologist begins by defining the concept to which the term refers in the source language. Firstly, he or she analyzes the source text, then broadens the analysis to other EU texts and then to other specialized texts in a given domain. If necessary, the terminologist may contact the persons responsible for the text and ask them for clarification. If the term is part of a bigger, central project, it is the central terminology unit that works out the concepts and supplements IATE with terms and definitions in the source language. On the basis of these definitions, the terminologists in the language departments can look for or create terms in their respective languages. When looking for equivalents of a term, the terminologist consults numerous bilingual sources, paper and electronic ones, chooses a possible equivalent in view of the reliability of such sources and checks the occurrence of this equivalent in various monolingual sources, over and over again, until he or she is finally happy with the result, which is then entered into IATE.

The majority of translators' questions[4] concern scientific terms from the domains under regulation. For example, the translator needs a Polish equivalent of the term *melting furnace*. The term comes from a Commission proposal establishing the Best Available Techniques (BAT) for non-ferrous metals. The definition for the English term is already available in IATE. The English-Polish Dictionary of Science and Technology (Berger et al. 2004: 692) suggests the equivalent *piec do topienia* [literally: furnance for melting]. Generally, dictionaries may be regarded as reliable sources; however, each source has to be treated critically and also dictionary terms are verified for their accuracy, adequacy and usage. Therefore, a simple internet query for the term *piec do topienia* is performed and it does not yield desirable results, i.e. no reliable texts where the term would be used in context are found. Some results are obtained only when the query is restricted to sites in the Polish language only and to the domain of metallurgy. One of the results of such a modified search is an article in a scientific journal, the title of which contains the term in question. The article is in Polish, but it contains an English version of the title with a slightly different term *piec topielny* [melting-ADJ furnance]. An internet query is performed again for the new term. It confirms the use of this term in specialized texts on reliable sites. Finally, the term *piec topielny* is entered into IATE.

[4]Approximately 90 per cent according to the internal statistics of DGT's Polish Language Department.

Such queries do not always yield expected results. The European Commission often regulates domains that are very specialized or novel. As a result, it happens that the terminology needed does not yet exist in the national languages or is not commonly spread or used by experts, who might prefer to communicate in English. Moreover, the available sources may be scarce or not reliable. This characteristics of EU terms may be illustrated with financial terms, such as *front running*, *capped notional value* or *LTROs*. In such a case the translator or the terminologist suggest possible equivalents according to their best knowledge and these suggestions are then consulted with national experts. Most language departments maintain contacts either with national administration of their Member State, or with experts in the Permanent Representation in Brussels, or even have direct contacts with specialists from various fields. When there is no time or possibility for such consultations, a descriptive equivalent is often used or a word-for-word (literal) equivalent, with the English term provided in brackets for extra clarity (the so-called translation couplet (cf. Newmark 1981: 32)). Such solutions are also often suggested by experts.

Literal translation is often criticized by text recipients in Member States. However, literal equivalents are a conscious technique used on purpose to minimize the risk of misinterpretation and to ensure consistency between all language versions. This concerns especially the so-called category A texts, where the lack of consistency may have legal consequences, i.e. EU legal documents; documents used in administrative or legal proceedings and inquiries, such as infringements or anti-dumping cases; documents for procurement or funding programmes, tenders, grants applications or contracts; as well as recruitment notices, EPSO (European Personnel Selection Office) competition notices and EPSO test documents (DGT 2017). For example, the term *vehicular language*, which might have been translated as *język roboczy* [working language], *język wspólny* [joint language] or *język uniwersalny* [universal language] in other contexts, was translated – upon the advice of the lawyer-linguists – literally, as *język wehikularny* in an EPSO competition notice, to avoid doubts as to which concept does this term refer to and to ensure consistency between all the language versions of the notice.

In particular **ambiguous terms** are most often translated literally. Word-for-word equivalents minimize the risk of future translation difficulties if a similar term were to appear to denote a different concept or if two terms that were synonymous at first had to be differentiated. For instance, the term *cross-zonal capacity* was first[5] translated as *transgraniczne zdolności przesyłowe* [literally: trans-

[5]Commission Regulation (EU) 2015/1222 of 24 July 2015 establishing a guideline on capacity allocation and congestion management (OJ L 197, 25.7.2015, p. 24–72).

border transfer capacity], because most of the bidding zones in Europe corresponded to the Members States' borders and the term was used interchangeably with the term *cross-border capacity.* It seemed a reasonable solution at that time; however, shortly afterwards, as a result of another act regulating the electricity market,[6] the responsible Directorate-General requested to keep the two terms apart. In consequence, the equivalent *transgraniczne zdolności przesyłowe* had to be changed by way of a corrigendum.[7] This could have been avoided if a more direct equivalent (*międzyobszarowe zdolności przesyłowe*) had been used from the very beginning.

Difficulties of another kind result from situations where a scientific term in the legal act to be translated is given a different meaning than it has in scientific discourse. This was the case with the terms *clinical study* and *clinical trial.* These two English terms refer to the same concept in medical texts and the equivalents *badanie kliniczne* or *próba kliniczna* can be used in Polish. However, Regulation 536/2014[8] started to use them as two distinct concepts, with *clinical trial* being defined as a category of *clinical study.* This made it necessary to distinguish these concepts in Polish by using terms that would take this difference into account to the greatest extent possible, while also taking into consideration the established and recognized Polish terminology in the field of clinical trials. After internal consultations the term *badanie kliniczne* [literally: clinical study] was kept as the equivalent of *clinical trial,* to maintain consistency with the terminology already established in Directive 2001/20/EC.[9] The term *badanie biomedyczne* [biomedical study] was used as the equivalent of *clinical study.* This term is not used in Polish law; hence, it was "empty" and it was possible to use it to denote the new concept.

Strictly legal terms do not occur in Commission texts that often, but when they do, they pose much greater difficulties than technical or scientific terms. The interpretation of legal terms, which are expressed in natural language, al-

[6]Commission Regulation (EU) 2016/1719 of 26 September 2016 establishing a guideline on forward capacity allocation (OJ L 259, 27.9.2016, p. 42–68).

[7]A corrigendum is a legal act, the purpose of which is to realign the published legislative text with the legislative body's original intent by removing obvious mistakes that occurred in the drafting and publication process (Bobek 2009: 950).

[8]Regulation (EU) No 536/2014 of the European Parliament and of the Council of 16 April 2014 on clinical trials on medicinal products for human use, and repealing Directive 2001/20/EC (OJ L 158, 27.5.2014, p. 1—76).

[9]Directive 2001/20/EC of the European Parliament and of the Council of 4 April 2001 on the approximation of the laws, regulations and administrative provisions of the Member States relating to the implementation of good clinical practice in the conduct of clinical trials on medicinal products for human use (OJ L 121, 1.5.2001, p. 34—44, special edition in Polish: Chapter 13 Volume 026 P. 299—309).

ways has to take into account the legal system in which they are used. This means that identically sounding terms belonging to different legal systems might have different meaning (e.g. terms in English in the English and American legal systems; terms in French in the French and Canadian legal systems; terms in German in the German and Austrian legal systems, etc.). The European Union also has its own specific legal system, although it does not have its own language and hence it has to "borrow" its legal terminology from the legal languages of the Member States (cf. Kjær 2007: 79, 80; Robertson 2010: 154). Still, it needs to be stressed that the concept system of EU law is distinct from that of the Member States because the EU legal system is distinct from the legal systems of EU Member States (cf. Case 282/81 *Srl CLIFIT and Lanificio di Gavardo SpA v Ministry of Health*). This distinction is the basis for the uniform application of EU law in all Member States and has to be accounted for in translation appropriately.

When translating from English (or more rarely French or other EU languages), the translator cannot be blinded by the meaning of the term in question in the English (or French) legal system, and during the search for equivalents, he or she has to be particularly cautious when borrowing terms from the national law.[10] This does not mean that using functional equivalents is not practiced; otherwise all translated terms would have to be neologisms. In particular, when the term is defined or when the context clearly points out to its "European" character, the functional equivalent may be good enough. For instance, the term *corruption* is translated simply as *korupcja*, although there is no single understanding of this concept that is common in all Members States (Szulik 2012). On the other hand, the translation of the term *identity card* with *dowód osobisty*, coming from the Polish Act on ID Cards,[11] would probably associate this term too much with the Polish legal system. In consequence, a less marked term *dowód tożsamości* is used.

Legal terms may be very specific and thus easily distinguishable, or they may be homonyms of everyday words that also have a specific meaning in the legal language (e.g. *goods*). Translators, who are for the most part not lawyers, may not be able to identify such terms properly; besides, not being experts, they have a tendency to use words in translation that are everyday equivalents of legal terms (e.g. *adopcja* instead of *przysposobienie* [adoption], Biel 2014: 273). A legal term may also be politically sensitive; in such a case, its equivalent may change whenever there is a change in the EU policy. Therefore, when the term

[10] Cf. e.g. point 5.3.2 of the *Joint practical guide of the European Parliament, the Council and the Commission*: "As regards legal terminology, terms which are too closely linked to a particular national legal system should be avoided." (European Union 2015: 18).

[11] Ustawa z dnia 6 sierpnia 2010 r. o dowodach osobistych (Dz.U. 2010 nr 167 poz. 1131).

illegal immigrant was changed to *irregular immigrant*, as the former started to be considered as stigmatizing, its translation in the Polish language versions of EU legislation also had to change from *nielegalny imigrant* to *imigrant o nieuregulowanym statusie.*

3 Criteria of translation choices

Translation is a decision-making process (cf. e.g.: Levý 1967). In the EU context, translators and terminologists make their choices based on three basic criteria: consistency, accuracy and clarity. Consistency refers to the lack of terminological discrepancies, accuracy means using correct and precise terms in a given context, and clarity is the degree to which the translation is understandable and fluent.

Above all, the target text has to be internally **consistent**. Consistency applies not only to terminology, but also to recurrent sentences and phrases; however, the consequence of the lack of terminological consistency tends to be much more serious. Various translations of the same term, especially in legal acts, may mislead the reader to think that these terms denote different concepts and make it difficult to interpret legislation. For the same reason translation has to be consistent with other EU legal acts, so that there is consistency within the EU legal order. Thus, the terminology in delegated or implementing acts has to be consistent with the terminology in the basic act while the terminology in the basic act has in turn to be consistent with the terminology in the primary legislation.

This means that when translating a regulation implementing a directive consistency has to be kept with the respective language version of that directive and not with the national legislation transposing it, even though it is the regulation that will be directly applicable in a given Member State. The Solvency II Directive is a good example.[12] The Polish Act on Insurance and Reinsurance activity,[13] which transposed the directive to the Polish law, changed or corrected many terms, e.g. *non-life insurance* was changed from *ubezpieczenia inne niż na życie* [literally: insurance other than life insurance] to *pozostałe ubezpieczenia osobowe i ubezpieczenia majątkowe* [literally: other personal insurance and property insurance]. The delegated regulation to this directive[14] is consistent with

[12]Directive 2009/138/EC of the European Parliament and of the Council of 25 November 2009 on the taking-up and pursuit of the business of Insurance and Reinsurance (Solvency II) (recast) (OJ L 335, 17.12.2009, p. 1–55).

[13]Ustawa z dnia 11 września 2015 r. o działalności ubezpieczeniowej i reasekuracyjnej (Dz.U. 2015 poz. 1844).

[14]Commission Delegated Regulation (EU) 2015/35 of 10 October 2014 supplementing Directive 2009/138/EC of the European Parliament and of the Council on the taking-up and pursuit of the business of Insurance and Reinsurance (Solvency II) (OJ L 12, 17.1.2015, p. 1–797).

the directive; however, it creates discrepancies between the Polish version of the regulation and the Polish transposing act, which are not easy to rectify as not every discrepancy is necessarily an error. It demonstrates that it is of utmost importance to ensure that the translation, especially the terminology, is right from the very beginning, and to maintain good contacts with national experts at each stage of the translation process.

Consistency is often more important than any other criterion. For example, during the translation of the proposal for a Directive on certain aspects concerning contracts for the online and other distance sales of goods[15] the translator had doubts about translating the key term – *sales of goods* – as *sprzedaż towarów* [literally: sale of goods]. When consulted, a Polish expert in the requesting Directorate-General suggested to use the term *sprzedaż rzeczy* [literally: sale of things]. The terminologist agreed with the expert on the accuracy of this equivalent; however, since the explanatory memorandum to the proposed Directive contained an explicit recommendation to keep the terminology consistent with the existing EU legislation, it was decided in the end to keep the equivalent *sprzedaż towarów*, to maintain consistency with Directive 2011/83/EU,[16] which the proposed Directive complemented, and where the term *goods* was defined and translated as *towary*.

The European Union does not produce 24 legal acts, but just one legal act in 24 language versions (Doczekalska 2009: 119–120). Therefore all language versions of an EU legal act must be consistent also between each other (which is referred to as **multilingual concordance**). In order to ensure this type of consistency to the greatest extent possible, translators cannot interfere with the structure of the source text, e.g. by splitting long sentences or rearranging paragraphs, nor can they correct any factual errors they spot in the source text, such as errors in numbers, even if they are obvious. They are asked to restrict their interpretation of the text to the actual wording of the source text. In the case of ambiguities in the source text, translators try to obtain clarifications from the person responsible for the text; such clarifications are then shared with translators in all other language departments (and other institutions, if necessary). However, ambiguities are very often used on purpose and translators are asked to keep them (cf. Šarčević 1997: 92–93). This is yet another reason for resorting to the literal translation technique (see above).

[15] COM(2015)0635 final.

[16] Directive 2011/83/EU of the European Parliament and of the Council of 25 October 2011 on consumer rights, amending Council Directive 93/13/EEC and Directive 1999/44/EC of the European Parliament and of the Council and repealing Council Directive 85/577/EEC and Directive 97/7/EC of the European Parliament and of the Council (OJ L 304, 22.11.2011, p. 64–88).

The second key criterion of translation choices is **accuracy**, both of specialized terms and of the EU-specific terminology. In the case of conflict between consistency and accuracy, it is usually consistency that prevails; however, each such case is examined separately. Quotations and clear references to a particular place in a legal act have to be cited verbatim, even if they contain outdated or incorrect terms, but it is still possible to correct spelling mistakes or apply the current spelling conventions in such quotations. In other cases, when the risk of misleading the reader as to which concept is meant is minimal, the use of correct terminology may be considered. For example, Regulation 1831/2003[17] contains the term *compounds of trace elements*, which was translated as *mieszanki pierwiastków śladowych* [literally: mixtures of trace elements], despite the fact that Polish law commonly uses the term *związki pierwiastków śladowych* [literally: compounds of trace elements]. Fortunately, it is not a legally defined term and it is only mentioned once as the name of one of the functional groups. Commission Implementing Regulations concerning authorizations to use certain substances as feed additives are regularly adopted on the basis of Regulation 1831/2003. According to the consistency criterion, the term from the basic regulation should be used in the corresponding implementing acts. However, implementing acts do not refer explicitly to the term in the basic act, and so in this particular context the correct term is used, even though it leads to inconsistencies with the basic regulation. In such situations, where no solution is perfect, solutions like this are considered "lesser evil" (Stefaniak 2013: 61).

Translation errors and discrepancies between language versions caused by them can be rectified by means of a **corrigendum**. However, in the case of corrigenda, too, one has to take into account the rule of consistency with the previous legislation and consider potential consequences that a corrigendum might have for legal acts already in force. The validity of each proposal to change terminology in an already published act is thoroughly investigated. For example, errors consisting in using a common word instead of a specialized term for the same concept do not qualify for a corrigendum. The use of the phrase *woreczek żółciowy* [literally: gall sack] as an equivalent of *gallbladder* is a mistake, because the right medical term in Polish is *pęcherzyk żółciowy* [literally: gall bladder]. However, the phrase *woreczek żółciowy* is widely understood and its use should not mislead the reader or have legal consequences. On the other hand, the terms *dokładność* [accuracy] and *precyzja* [precision], which seem to be synonymous, have very

[17] Regulation (EC) No 1831/2003 of the European Parliament and of the Council of 22 September 2003 on additives for use in animal nutrition (OJ L 268, 18.10.2003, p. 29–43, Special edition in Polish: Chapter 03 Volume 040 P. 238–252).

different meaning in analytical chemistry and cannot be used interchangeably in this context. Therefore, the use of the term *dokładność* as an equivalent of *precision* would be a serious mistake that requires a corrigendum.

The third criterion taken into account when making terminological decisions is **clarity**. When striving for clarity, the quality of the source text is of key importance. Unfortunately, the majority of EU texts intended for translation are not written by native speakers; moreover, they are a result of negotiations on various political levels and hence a compromise. The lack of a single author and the necessity to satisfy the needs and wishes of many parties engaged in the drafting process increase, inter alia, the tendency for generalizations and stylistic neutrality (Koskinen 2008), making the text less clear. Moreover, the drafting phase and the translation phase often overlap, and in consequence the translator receives a text that is not a final version of the legal act and is still being drafted (cf. Doczekalska 2009; Stefaniak 2013). In other words, translators have to deal with many versions of the same text: some elements are deleted, others are added, concepts are redefined and terminology is changed. Many changes to the original version of the source text also result from translators' comments, who notice mistakes or make suggestions for improvements, but for the sake of multilingual concordance are not allowed to correct them by themselves without a new version.

Because of the above mentioned factors, which are independent of the translator, and because of the necessity to maintain above all the consistency and accuracy of translation, translators have very limited possibility to influence the clarity of their texts. This also means that the textual fit of national language versions of EU legal acts, i.e. a degree to which these legal acts depart from the conventions of legal acts originally written in a given language (neutrality of translation), is considered to be divergent for the Polish language (Biel 2014: 289–292). It is, however, hardly surprising. EU translators are expected to create texts which are comprehensible, linguistically correct and terminologically accurate, and at the same time consistent with EU legislation and with other language versions, and on top of that able to fit in the national legislation. Creating a translation that fulfils these contradictory expectations is practically impossible.

4 Conclusions

Terminology errors have particularly serious consequences for citizens and business entities, who usually rely only on one language version and thus can misunderstand their rights and obligations. Discrepancies between language versions[18] make the harmonization, interpretation and application of EU legislation more difficult, may lead to court proceedings on the national or Union level, lower the trust of citizens towards the EU and undermine the image of EU institutions. This attracts the interest of all EU institutions' translation services in the terminology work and its integration in the translation process. Of course, the right terminology alone does not guarantee high-quality translation, but it is difficult to imagine good translation without the right terminology.

References

Berger, Maria M., Teresa Jaworska, Anna Baranowska & Monika Barańska (eds.). 2004. *Słownik naukowo-techniczny angielsko-polski [English-Polish scientific and technical dictionary].* Warszawa: Wydawnictwa Naukowo-Techniczne.

Biel, Łucja. 2014. *Lost in the Eurofog: the textual fit of translated law.* Frankfurt am Main: Peter Lang.

Bobek, Michal. 2009. Corrigenda in the Official Journal of the European Union: Community law as quicksand. *European Law Review* 34. 950–962.

Directorate-General for Translation (DGT), European Commission. 2012. *Quantifying quality costs and the cost of poor quality in translation. quality efforts and the consequences of poor quality in the European Commission's Directorate-General for Translation.* Luxembourg: Publications Office of the European Union.

Directorate-General for Translation (DGT), European Commission. 2017. *Translation quality info sheet for contractors.* https://ec.europa.eu/info/sites/info/files/freelance_info_en.pdf, accessed 2017-9-19.

Doczekalska, Agnieszka. 2009. Drafting or translation: production of multilingual legal texts. In Francis Olsen, Alexander Lorz & Dieter Stein (eds.), *Translation issues in language and law*, 116–135. Basingstoke: Palgrave MacMillan.

European Union. 2015. *Joint practical guide of the European Parliament, the Council and the Commission for persons involved in the drafting of European Union legislation.* Luxembourg.

ISO 1087-1:2000. 2000. *Terminology work – Vocabulary – Part 1: Theory and application.* Geneva: ISO.

[18] Of course, not all translation errors are errors in terminology, however, in as much as 84 per cent of cases dealt with by the Court of Justice that involved discrepancy between language versions the discrepancy concerned terminology (DGT 2012: 28).

ISO 9000:2015. 2015. *Quality management systems – Fundamentals and vocabulary.* Geneva: ISO.

Kjær, Anne Lise. 2007. Legal translation in the European Union: A research field in need of a new approach. In Krzysztof Kredens & Stanisław Goźdź-Roszkowski (eds.), *Language and the law: international outlooks*, 69–95. Frankfurt am Main: Peter Lang.

Koskinen, Kaisa. 2008. *Translating institutions. an ethnographic study of EU translation.* Manchester: St. Jerome.

Levý, Jiří. 1967. Translation as a decision process. In, vol. 2, 1171–1182. The Hague: Mouton.

Newmark, Peter. 1981. *Approaches to translation.* London/New York: Prentice Hall.

Robertson, Colin. 2010. EU law and semiotics. *International Journal for the Semiotics of Law* 23. 145–164.

Šarčević, Susan. 1997. *New approach to legal translation.* The Hague: Kluwer Law International.

Stefaniak, Karolina. 2013. Multilingual legal drafting, translators' choices and the principle of lesser evil. *Meta. The Translators' Journal* 58(1). 58–65.

Szulik, Marcin. 2012. Analiza unijnych rozwiązań legislacyjnych w zakresie prawa antykorupcyjnego [Analysis of EU legislative solution in the field of anticorruption law]. In Jerzy Kosiński, Krzysztof Kraka & Anna Koman (eds.), *Korupcja i antykorupcja. wybrane zagadnienia [corruption and anitcorruption. selected issues]*, 11–58. Warszawa: Wydział Wydawnictw i Poligrafii Centrum Szkolenia Policji.

Chapter 7

Evaluation of outsourced translations. State of play in the European Commission's Directorate-General for Translation (DGT)

Ingemar Strandvik

Directorate-General for Translation, European Commission*

The European Commission's Directorate-General for Translation (DGT), with its 1,500 in-house translators, produces yearly over 2 million pages of institutional translation and multilingual law. Over the last years, the mounting pressure for cost-efficiency has triggered a detailed scrutiny of all workflow processes and led to staff reductions combined with an increased use of outsourcing. This chapter presents how DGT has put in place a corporate quality management policy, approaching quality not only as product quality but also as quality of processes. It describes how focus on needs and expectations naturally led to highlighting the key role of purpose for text production, defining translation quality as fitness-for-purpose, in line with applicable standards. Furthermore, it shows how DGT in order to operationalise this definition addressed various other issues and questions. The outcome was translation quality guidelines outlining the communicative purposes of different text categories and the risks involved. In the implementation of the guidelines, there has been a perceived tension between the fitness-for-purpose concept and high quality, on the one hand, and between the fitness-for-purpose concept and the traditional fidelity paradigm, on the other. The paper analyses why this tension is only apparent and why the fitness-for-purpose concept better than the traditional fidelity concept caters for the needs of the institutional translation and multilingual law-making that takes place in the European context.

*The author is Quality Manager in DGT. The opinions expressed are those of the author and should not be considered as representing the European Commission's official position.

Ingemar Strandvik. 2017. Evaluation of outsourced translations. State of play in the European Commission's Directorate-General for Translation (DGT). in Tomáš Svoboda, Łucja Biel & Krzysztof Łoboda (eds.), *Quality aspects in institutional translation*, 123–137. Berlin: Language Science Press. DOI:10.5281/zenodo.1048194

1 Introduction

The European Commission is the executive body of the European Union. It implements the European policies, it proposes new legislation and monitors that EU law is applied correctly by the Member States. All these activities are carried out and communicated in 24 official languages with an equal status. This means that multilingualism is at the heart of the EU. The resulting massive translation demand was formerly met almost exclusively through in-house translation. However, after the number of official languages has increased over the years, with successive enlargements, in particular the "big bang" enlargement in 2004, when 9 new official languages were added to the then 11, and as translation volumes have continued to grow, more and more translations are now outsourced, both in pursuit of cost-efficiency and due to insufficient internal capacity. All in all, the number of in-house translators in the pre-enlargement languages has been reduced by almost 50 per cent over the last twenty years, but with the arrival of the new languages, the total number of translators in the Directorate-General for Translation (DGT) of the European Commission has remained roughly the same. Today, with 24 official languages, there are some 1,500 in-house translators and DGT translates over 2 million pages per year for the European Commission, roughly a third of which are supplied by external contractors via outsourcing.

This article aims at describing how DGT has organised its outsourcing operations. In particular, it focuses on evaluation principles and practices and some of the challenges involved.

2 Outsourcing and evaluation

To outsource these considerable volumes, DGT relies on multiple framework contracts with a dynamic ranking system. The system features a tendering procedure where the quality/price ratio has been put at 70/30. It also features systematic evaluation, where a 10 per cent sample of each translation is revised, assessed and marked using a five-grade scale.[1] The mark affects the contractor's position in the dynamic ranking, which in turn influences how assignments are distributed.

As the proportion of outsourcing has increased considerably over the years, streamlining outsourcing has become a real issue, to achieve both cost-efficient work organisation and equal treatment of hundreds of external contractors. Moreover, since DGT today outsources all types of documents, including draft legislation and high-profile policy documents, it has become crucial to ensure that

[1] "Very good" (10), "Good" (8), "Below standard" (6), "Insufficient" (4) and "Unacceptable" (0).

outsourcing does not have a negative impact on quality. To this end, the tender specifications of the most recent call for tenders for outsourced translations (OMNIBUS-15, in place since 1 July 2016) included the following quality requirements:

> The quality of the translations must be such that they can be used as they stand upon delivery, without any further formatting, revision, review and/or correction by the contracting authority. To this end, the contractor must thoroughly revise and review the entire target text, ensuring inter alia that:
>
> - it is complete (without unjustified omissions or additions);
> - it is an accurate and consistent rendering of the source text;
> - references to documents already published have been checked and quoted correctly;
> - the terminology and lexis are consistent with any relevant reference material and internally;
> - appropriate attention has been paid to the clarity and register and text-type conventions;
> - it contains no syntactical, spelling, punctuation, typographical, grammatical or other errors;
> - the formatting of the original has been maintained (including codes and tags if applicable);
> - any specific instructions given by the authorising department are followed; and
> - the agreed deadline (date and time) is scrupulously respected.

Evaluation plays a key role to ascertain whether these quality requirements have been complied with. To evaluate linguistic and textual quality, all outsourced translations are assessed on the basis of the evaluation grid in table 1 below.

Identified errors are further classified according to their severity as 'low-relevance' or 'high-relevance' errors. A high-relevance error is defined as an error that seriously impairs the usability of the text for its intended purpose. Moreover, evaluators assess whether the product delivery (including translation memories, etc.) is complete, whether DGT's instructions have been followed and whether the formatting requirement and set deadlines have been complied with. If this is not the case, separate penalties apply.

Table 1: Evaluation grid currently used by DGT

Error type	Code	Relevance Low	Relevance High	Error type	Code	Relevance Low	Relevance High
Mistranslation, unjustified addition	SENS			Reference docs/material not used; norm sources or job-specific instructions not adhered to	RD		
Unjustified omission or non-translation	OM			Wrong or inconsistent EU usage or terminology	TERM		
Clarity, register and text-type conventions	CL			Punctuation	PT		
Grammar	GR			Spelling	SP		

The evaluation is carried out by the in-house translators, who are expected to possess the competence needed to evaluate outsourced translations. Evaluations, just like translations and revisions, are assigned on the basis of the competence profiles of the available staff.

3 Issues in the past

Under the former framework contract GEN-11 – which applied from 1 July 2012 to 1 July 2016 – the system worked rather well and the performance improved over the contract period, partly because of the feedback given to the contractors to clarify DGT's needs and expectations as regards quality. Having said that, some issues related to evaluation were considered to be problematic. The main issues identified were consistency of evaluations and the high cost of administration and contract management.

Consistency of evaluation practices and results is inevitably a challenge when 1,500 in-house translators are expected to be able to carry out translation quality assessments in a uniform and supposedly repeatable manner. Translation is constant decision-making. It is about constantly making choices. As Pym (1992) puts it, there are binary translation errors (choices that are correct or incorrect) and non-binary ones (choices that are not necessarily right or wrong but more or less appropriate). The problem for translators, revisers and evaluators alike is that most quality issues are of the non-binary type. To assess quality consistently you need to be clear about why some choices are better than others. When operating in an institutional translation setting of DGT's scale, this obviously becomes an issue.

Moreover, it is a fact that freelance markets are different. The freelance markets in the German language area with a population of 100 million people, the Estonian with around a million, or the Maltese with some 450,000 are not the same in terms of capacity, specialisation and maturity. This inevitably has an effect on consistency in the approaches to how to interact with the markets.

As to the management and administration costs, in principle, according to the outsourcing framework contract, the translations received were supposed to be usable as they stood upon delivery, without any further intervention from DGT, other than the evaluation of the 10 per cent sample applied to all outsourced texts. Despite this, two thirds of the outsourced pages were further quality controlled in-house i.e. beyond the 10 per cent. This appeared to be a failure cost, considering that almost 95 per cent of the translations still received the pass marks "very good" or "good". It was asked why DGT should spend in-house resources to revising texts that had already been revised by the contractor and that were marked "very good" or "good", which should mean they are usable as such.

The inquiries into why this happened showed several things. First, that the time allocated for the task of evaluating a page amounted to 10 per cent of the time allocated for the task of translation, while the conversion rate for the task revision was 40 per cent of a translated page. Since evaluation consists of *revising* a 10 per cent sample, this meant that carrying out a thorough evaluation, mechanically led to spending more time than what was accounted for, thereby lowering internal productivity and further increasing the difference in costs for internally and externally produced pages. This led to instances where evaluation was based on a less thorough revision of the sample, giving the external translator the benefit of the doubt, applying an overly lenient marking.

Second, it appeared that often the additional revision was done because of the type of document concerned and the risks involved. When higher-risk documents such as strategic communications, articles for publication, or draft legislation were outsourced, language departments did not dare to rely solely on a spot check. For the sake of comparison, it could be mentioned that the translation department of the European Court of Justice contends that when they outsource the translation of court rulings, they revise the entire outsourced text, even if it has been revised by the contractor according to the contract, because it produces legal effects and the translation departments need to ensure that the legal effects are correct. If only parts of the document are revised, this cannot be guaranteed.

Third, it was also found that in many language departments it was the *usefulness* of the translation that was assessed rather than its *usability*. As mentioned above, the overall quality requirement according to the tender specifications is that the text delivered should be usable as it stands. However, even in cases where the entire text needed revision, modifications and corrections, outsourced translations were regularly considered to be clearly *useful* for the finalisation of the text – and therefore "very good" or at least "good". Finally, instances were also identified where evaluators awarded good marks as a reflection of their empathy with freelance translators and their (assumably) less favourable working conditions.

4 Developing quality guidelines and the notion of quality

Traditionally in the EU context, when someone passes a recruitment test – a competition – for a post as translator, it is taken for granted that he or she has the competences needed to translate, revise, evaluate translation quality and carry out terminological work. At the same time, for many languages translators were recruited without formal studies in translation, since in many cases such studies did not exist at the time of accession of their country (Biel 2011, Strandvik 2014). If we add to that the sheer number of the people involved, it is clear that a major challenge has always been – and is likely to always be – to ensure that the institution speaks with one voice, not only when translating and revising, but also when evaluating outsourced translations. What has been done to address this issue?

In a major quality management project called *Programme for Quality Management in Translation – 22 Quality Actions* (DGT 2009), DGT set up a number of working groups to analyse 22 quality-related topics and processes relevant for the quality of the translation services provided. Several of these actions were related to outsourcing and evaluation, for instance actions aiming to improve translation briefs and feedback for freelancers and develop standards for the evaluation of freelance translations (including specific training, error quantification and tools for evaluation).

As a result of these initiatives, apart from a series of language-specific revision workshops and quality control guidelines, common guidelines for evaluation of outsourced translation were issued in 2009 (cf. DGT 2013). Moreover, a quality assessment tool based on the LISA QA model (cf. Doherty & Gaspari 2013) and attributing penalty points for errors was introduced, on the basis of the widely spread belief that translation quality had to be measured with analytical, and not holistic quality assessment. However, at the time, only five language departments found the error quantifying tool useful. Not surprisingly, one of the main objections was that in order for quality assessment to be consistent (so called inter-rater reliability), there needs to be a common understanding of the principles for evaluation and of the error categorisations and severity levels used. Otherwise, the objectivity of the assessment tool is reduced to an objective calculation of error points resulting from a subjective identification of errors.

Indeed, over the years, in different internal contexts, there has been a growing awareness about the fact that a pre-requisite for any institutional attempts to speak with one consistent voice in translation, revision and evaluation is that there is a shared understanding of what is actually meant by quality. Around 2012, it appeared that while everybody agreed to DGT's mission statement that DGT should provide the Commission with high-quality translation, there was no common definition of what DGT meant by high-quality translation. Time was ripe to come up with such a definition and develop a more structured approach to quality management. This resulted in *DGT's Quality management framework* (DGT 2014), a steering document for quality management in which quality is defined as fitness-for-purpose and key processes are described. The definition adopted reads:

> A translation is fit for purpose when it is suitable for its intended communicative use and satisfies the expressed or implied needs and expectations of our direct customers (requesting DGs), our partners in the other EU institutions, the end-users and any other relevant stakeholders.
>
> Consequently, fitness for purpose means high quality in the abovementioned sense. It should not be mixed up with the good-enough quality concept used by the software industry and in the machine translation context. The fitness for purpose concept is at the core of DGT's internal quality control (QC) guidelines (Consolidated guidelines on quality control) and of the Service Level agreements (SLAs) DGT has signed with other DGs.

With this definition, DGT boldly aims at reclaiming the fitness-for-purpose concept to mean suitability for the intended purpose, in line with the logic of all professional standards, and not "good enough quality" as it has been defined for example by TAUS (TAUS EUG Resolution #2).

To operationalise the fitness-for-purpose principle, common translation quality guidelines (DGT 2015) were then issued. They describe the different purposes of different types of EU documents, explain potential risks caused by deficient quality and provide text type specific instructions for translation and quality control, based on risk assessment. These developments and DGT's reference model for quality management (Figure 1) are described in detail in Strandvik (2017) and Drugan et al. (2018)).

Figure 1: DGT's Reference model for translation quality management.

5 From fidelity to fitness-for-purpose

During the last 15 years, a pragmatic, functionalist approach to specialised translation has made its way into the standards of the profession. Successively, the German DIN-2345:1998-04, the European EN 15038:2006 , the American ASTM F2575, and ISO/TS 11669:2012, ISO 17100:2015 all clearly state that extra-linguistic aspects such as specifications (or briefs) are key for quality, revision is defined as assessing a translation as to its suitability for the intended purpose, which is to say that the purpose and the specifications are the yardstick against which you determine the appropriateness of the translation choices. Indeed, in service provision, quality is defined as compliance with requirements. Translation service provision is no exception: translation quality is compliance with requirements, it is not just faithfulness to the original. The reason why the functionalists made their way into the standards is that their theories work in practice and make sense, not only for translators but for all the stakeholders involved.

This move from fidelity to fitness-for-purpose has taken place not only in DGT but also in the other EU institutions (see for instance the contribution from the Council in this volume). This is logical if translation is approached as professional drafting and as communication acts. Any text can be improved. Most texts drafted for professional purposes contain imperfections and even errors, without being unfit for their purpose. The same applies to professional translation.

As spelled out in the DGT Translation quality guidelines, the European Commission has issued a number of drafting guidelines to explain to drafters how it wants to communicate and what it wants to achieve when communicating through different text types. This communicative intent is not limited to the source text and should be fulfilled also through the 23 translated official language versions. Therefore, translators should be familiar with these guidelines to apply them to the extent possible when translating. This is all the more important as today there is hardly ever any in-depth editing after translation, not even for legal acts (Guggeis & Robinson 2012: 62, Strandvik 2014). The translated texts should stand on their own. According to constant case law, once an EU legal act is adopted, there are no originals and no translations, only equally authentic language versions. And as Husa puts it (2012: 179), what matters in legal translation is not what the texts say linguistically, but what they say legally.

DGT has witnessed this evolution also in its evaluation practices. Formerly, the severity level "high relevance" was defined with a reference to a change in meaning (a high relevance spelling error was a spelling error that changed the meaning), whereas now, as explained above, a high relevance error is defined as an error which "seriously impairs the usability of the text". Exactly the same error can be of high or low relevance not because it affects the meaning but because it affects the usability of the text differently. A spelling mistake in a 15-page text is likely to be a non-issue, whereas if it appears on a poster in big letters it could be fatal. A wrong date appearing on page 55 in a report could be insignificant, whereas the date of entry into force of a legal act or the date and time of a meeting are crucial, etc. A mistranslation in the enacting terms of a legal act is likely to affect the usability of the text, whereas exactly the same mistranslation in the explanatory memorandum is less likely to have that effect. Formerly, the quality requirements in tender specifications stated that the contractor should provide a faithful rendering of the source text and eliminate any discrepancies between the source and the target text. Now, as quoted above, they state that the text should be an "accurate and consistent rendering of the source text". Discrepancies is an unclear concept. Discrepancies as to denotation, connotation, text-type convention, pragmatics or form? Discrepancies are, in fact, sometimes required to comply with the formal style guides for legislative drafting for different languages, or to make a web text read smoothly, or to make a text fit to a button on screen.

Moving towards an understanding of quality that could be shared and embraced by 1,500 translators from 28 different national contexts with very different professional and educational backgrounds, working in 24 different language departments, is a challenge. If we scratch the surface, there are still different conceptual understandings of what translation is. One which embraces the functionalist approach to translation (fidelity to the purpose of the communication) seeing the translators as active and competent drafters of the equally authentic translated language versions of texts with a function, and another which embraces the idea of faithfulness (fidelity to the source text's surface structure) as the main criterion for translation quality, seeing the translators as "just translators", where their task is limited to the faithful rendering of the "original" in the target text.

These perceptions seem to be deeply anchored in beliefs and values. It would be interesting to explore this further: Is it a divide between experienced and unexperienced translators? Or between translators with and without formal studies in translation? Is it linked to age? Is it the accuracy requirements of legal translation that contaminate all other aspects of translation? Are there different national translation cultures? Does it have to do with administrative culture and institutional power relations affecting the translators' agency? Some translators naturally interact with requesters and national experts for clarifications, whereas some rather do not. The latter, do they "hide" behind the source text?

Melby et al. (2014) and Koby et al. (2014) address this issue in an interesting way, with reference to discussions at FIT's World Congress 2014 on the relation between localization/transcreation and translation, suggesting a distinction between different beliefs on what translation is (Melby et al. 2014: 392–403) and what translation quality is (Koby et al. 2014: 413–420).

6 Recent developments and further challenges

To cope with the increase in outsourcing, and to ensure a streamlined and consistent workflow, a new Outsourcing framework was adopted in 2016. Furthermore, in view of the new framework contract OMNIBUS-15, which entered into force on 1 July 2016, new evaluation guidelines were drafted to address the abovementioned issues.

The *DGT Outsourcing framework* (DGT 2016b) puts emphasis on supplier management. It aims to improve the quality of outsourced translations through improved communication: via meetings with the suppliers, better specifications linked to the Translation quality guidelines and systematic and more harmonized feedback. Even if the quality requirements in the new framework contract (quoted above) have remained the same as before, the new evaluation guidelines, *DGT Guidelines for evaluation of outsourced translation* (DGT 2016a) introduced some novelties: the link between evaluation and the quality requirements of the tender specifications was made clearer. Definitions were added to the marks. It was also clarified that the evaluation is above all a contractual obligation for payment clearance, not as such a reliable quality control measure for risk mitigation. In other words, its result which is based on a 10 per cent spot check does not guarantee the intrinsic quality of the entire text. To address the issue of additional quality control applied after outsourcing, it was decided that the Translation quality guidelines apply to all translation, whether produced externally or internally. The result of the evaluation therefore feeds into the global risk assessment. A poor evaluation result is likely to trigger extended quality control, according to the escalation principle, whereas a very good result could lead to stopping the effort after the evaluation of 10 per cent. At the same time, depending on the risks involved, it can be decided that regardless of the result of the evaluation, the entire document, for instance speeches and binding legislation, should undergo full revision. Moreover, to ensure a consistent approach to marking, systematic *validation* of all marks was introduced, with a limited number of validators checking all evaluation results for consistency (but not re-doing the evaluations).

Current evaluation challenges further include sharing practices across languages on where to draw the line between the two severity levels (high and low relevance errors) and where to put the thresholds between the different marks, and how to harmonise feedback comments in a way that is consistent with the tender specifications and the definitions of the marks. Another challenge is to finetune the sampling practices. In the EU institutions and in industry practices range from industrial sampling based on the ISO 2859-1 standard to full in-house revision. We are still lacking empirical evidence as to the reliability of quality assessment based on different sample sizes. Is 10 per cent reliable? Is 20 per cent more reliable?

With the new quality management structure, and a more common understanding of quality, time has also been deemed ripe for a new attempt to consider introducing a tool to further streamline the quality assessment of outsourced translations. DGT is currently testing different existing tools and assessment models and follows closely the ongoing standardisation initiatives of ISO and ASTM as well as the EU funded QT21 project, and the resulting Multidimensional quality metrics (MQM).[2] The outcome of those initiatives are likely to lead to an updating of the error categorisation and of the weightings currently used.

7 Conclusions

The experience gained in DGT over the years shows that we cannot translate, revise or evaluate translation quality in a consistent way, if we do not have a shared understanding of translation quality. With so many actors, it is important to state the quality requirements explicitly, to avoid misunderstandings and miscommunication. The reference model for translation quality management recently put in place in DGT is a useful step on the long and winding road towards this long-term objective.

In this endeavour, DGT is increasingly relying on international standardisation efforts. The very purpose of standardisation is to identify and define key concepts, to ensure seamless communication, and to establish and prescribe workflow steps, so that all stakeholders know what to expect from each other when interacting in relation to the standardised activity. Standards represent the distilled wisdom of the profession. Even if DGT doesn't need translation standards for certification purposes, referring to them for benchmarking purposes has become a means to improve working methods and communication.

One emerging key question in that context is what kind of competence profile is needed to be able to evaluate translations. Is it the same as for revision, e.g. in terms of subject matter competence? A very important related question is: How much can we outsource? Is there a tipping point after which the European Commission will no longer be in control of its communication and legislative drafting because it no longer has the in-house domain competence to assess and ensure quality?

---

[2]http://www.qt21.eu/quality-metrics/

The administration of contracts is expensive. Ideas to elicit savings often end up being costly, creating hidden costs that put strain on the in-house staff. Attempts to apply industrial (and much cheaper) sampling methods have so far been problematic and not given satisfactory results. As with any service provision, what really matters is to specify the quality requirements. What text quality does the European Commission need and who is responsible for ensuring this quality? The question is perhaps not whether the European Commission can afford to quality control outsourced translations but rather whether it can afford not to do it.

References

ASTM F2575. 2014. *14 Standard Guide for Quality Assurance in Translation.* West Conshohocken.

Biel, Łucja. 2011. Training translators or translation service providers? EN 15038:2006 standard of translation services and its training implications. *JoS-Trans: The Journal of Specialised Translation* 16. 61–76.

DIN-2345:1998-04. 1998. *Übersetzungsaufträge.* Berlin.

Directorate-General for Translation (DGT), European Commission. 2009. *Programme for Quality Management in Translation – 22 Quality Actions.* http://translationjournal.net/e-Books/programme-for-quality-management-in-translation.html, accessed 2017-9-30.

Directorate-General for Translation (DGT), European Commission. 2013. *Document quality control in public administrations and international organisations.* Luxembourg.

Directorate-General for Translation (DGT), European Commission. 2014. *DGT Quality Management Framework. Ares(2014)799428 [internal document].*

Directorate-General for Translation (DGT), European Commission. 2015. *DGT translation quality guidelines.* http://ec.europa.eu/translation/maltese/guidelines/documents/dgt_translation_quality_guidelines_en.pdf, accessed 2017-8-24.

Directorate-General for Translation (DGT), European Commission. 2016a. *Management plan 2016. DGT. Ref. Ares(2016)2103398 - 03/05/201.* https://ec.europa.eu/info/sites/info/files/management-plan-2016-dg-dgt-may2016_en.pdf, accessed 2017-7-1.

Directorate-General for Translation (DGT), European Commission. 2016b. *Strategic plan 2016-2020. DG Translation. Ref. Ares(2016)1329034 - 16/03/201.* https://

ec.europa.eu/info/sites/info/files/strategic-plan-2016-2020-dg-t_march2016_en.pdf, accessed 2017-7-1.

Doherty, Stephen & Federico Gaspari. 2013. *Understanding and implementing effective translation quality evaluation techniques. QTLaunchpad.* http://www.qt21.eu/launchpad/sites/default/files/QTLP%20GALA%20Webinar%203.pdf, accessed 2017-9-30.

Drugan, Joanna, Ingemar Strandvik & Erkka Vuorinen. 2018. Translation quality, quality management and agency: principles and practice in the European Union institutions. In Joss Moorkens, Sheila Castilho, Stephen Doherty & Federico Gaspari (eds.), *Translation quality assessment: from principles to practice.* Berlin: Springer.

Guggeis, Manuela & William Robinson. 2012. 'co-revision': legal-linguistic revison in the European Union 'co-decision' process. In C. J. W. Baaij (ed.), *The role of legal translation in legal harmonization*, 51–81. The Hague: Kluwer Law International.

Husa, Jaakko. 2012. Understanding legal languages. linguistic concerns of the comparative lawyer. In C. J. W. Baaij (ed.), *The Role of Legal Translation in Legal Harmonisation*, 161–181. The Hague: Kluwer Law International.

ISO 17100:2015. 2015. *Translation services – Requirements for translation services.* Geneva: ISO. http://www.iso.org/iso/catalogue_detail.htm?csnumber=59149.

ISO 2859-1. 2006. *Sampling procedures. Part 1: Sampling schemes indexed by acceptable quality limit (AQL) for lot-by-lot inspection.* Geneva: ISO.

ISO/TS 11669:2012. 2012. *Translation projects – General guidance.* Geneva: ISO.

Koby, Geoffrey S., Paul Fields, Daryl Hague, Arle Lommel & Alan Melby. 2014. Defining translation quality. *Tradumàtica* 12. 413–420.

Melby, Alan, Paul Fields, Daryl Hague, Geoffrey S. Koby & Arle Lommel. 2014. Defining the landscape of translation. *Tradumàtica* 12. 392–403.

Pym, Anthony. 1992. Translation error analysis and the interface with language teaching. In C. Dollerup & A. Loddegaard (eds.), *The teaching of translation*, 279–288. Amsterdam: John Benjamins.

for Standardization (CEN), European Committee. 2006. *EN 15038:2006 Translation services – service requirements.* Brussels: CEN.

Strandvik, Ingemar. 2014. Is there scope for a more professional approach to EU multilingual lawmaking? *The Theory and Practice of Legislation* 2(2). 211–228.

Strandvik, Ingemar. 2017. Towards a more structured approach to quality assurance: DGT's quality journey. In Fernando Prieto Ramos (ed.), *Institutional translation for international governance: enhancing quality in multilingual legal communication*, 51–62. London: Bloomsbury.

TAUS. 2017. *TAUS DQF Enterprise user group. Topic #2: DQF Quality levels resolution.* https://www.taus.net/file-downloads/download-file?path=DQF%2FEUG_Resolution-2_QualityLevels.pdf, accessed 2017-9-30.

Chapter 8

Quality assurance at the Council of the EU's Translation Service

Jan Hanzl

John Beaven

Council of the European Union*

The aim of this chapter is to describe quality assurance mechanisms at the Translation Service of the General Secretariat of the Council of the EU (GSC). The first part will put the GSC's translation activity into a more general framework of the workings of the whole institution. Furthermore, the GSC's approach to translation quality will be explained, and tools and procedures that are used and help translators achieve the required quality of their products will be described. The next part will focus on the ex-post quality monitoring that was introduced a few years ago to systematically monitor both the quality of translations that leave the Translation Service and the individual performance of translators. The final part will be dedicated to a recently-adopted special procedure to ensure the best quality of the GSC Translation Service's hallmark product – the European Council conclusions. The chapter is descriptively oriented and draws on everyday practice of a GSC's translator and the quality policy coordinator. Hopefully, it will raise awareness of the activities of the GSC's Translation Service, provide inspiration for other translation departments and practitioners and offer topics for further research for academia.

With approximately 600 translators and 300 other management and support staff, the General Secretariat of the Council of the EU's Translation Service is a little smaller than the European Parliament's Directorate-General for Translation and about half the size of the European Commission's Directorate-General for Translation, but still large by most standards. Each year the Council's service translates around 15,000 documents, which represent roughly 110,000 pages of source material and a yearly translation output, expressed as a sum of all target languages, in

*The views expressed are our own and in no way reflect the views of the Council or the European Council.

Jan Hanzl & John Beaven. 2017. Quality assurance at the Council of the EU's Translation Service. In Tomáš Svoboda, Łucja Biel & Krzysztof Łoboda (eds.), *Quality aspects in institutional translation*, 139–153. Berlin: Language Science Press. DOI:10.5281/zenodo.1048196

the range of 1.2 million pages (Council of the European Union, General Secretariat (2016b), Council of the European Union, General Secretariat (2017)). However, quality rather than quantity has always been the primary focus of the Council's Translation Service, and the aim of this chapter is to describe the quality assurance mechanisms that are used at the Council's Translation Service to ensure the required quality of its products.

1 The Council(s), the General Secretariat of the Council and its Translation Service

To understand the approach to translation quality at the General Secretariat of the Council of the EU's Translation Service, it is necessary to put its translation activity into a more general framework of the workings of the two institutions it serves, namely the Council of the European Union, formerly known as the Council of Ministers, where ministers meet to adopt legislation and coordinate policies, and the European Council, which brings together the heads of state or government in meetings also known as EU Summits. Since the Lisbon Treaty, these two Councils are formally two EU institutions, but both are supported by one general secretariat – the General Secretariat of the Council (GSC) – of which the Translation Service is a part. The Translation Service itself is split into 24 units, one per official language. Each language unit usually consists of just over 20 translators, a Head of Unit, a Quality Controller and a number of assistants. Most of the time, translators work into their mother tongue, and the language of source documents is predominantly English.[1]

Still, the Councils themselves are only the tip of an iceberg for the GSC Translation Service's work. Underneath, there are more than 150 specialized Working Parties and Committees which discuss and prepare the documents before their formal adoption. As the flow of documents through this structure of preparatory bodies up to the Councils themselves has major implications for the translation work, it deserves a brief description. Most EU legislation originates with a proposal from the Commission, presented in all 24 EU official languages. This proposal is discussed, often several times, by Member States' experts at relevant Working Parties. The experts usually make changes to the source-language version of the text, and, at certain point, the amended text is sent to the Translation Service for translation. Then the same process may be repeated at the same or higher level preparatory body, until there is sufficient support from all Member

[1] In 2016, well over 90 % of all translations at the GSC were done from English (Council of the European Union, General Secretariat 2017).

States and the text can be submitted to the Council for approval. In the case of legislative acts, the text is subsequently sent for finalization to lawyer-linguists from the GSC's Legal Service. In reality, the whole process is much more complicated, but the aim of this simplified description is to illustrate why translators' work at the GSC predominantly looks as shown in Figure 1.

This document comparison is produced with a standard commercial tool (Workshare Compare) and shows what has changed since the last translated version: additions are shown in blue, deletions in red and moved text in green. The task of GSC's translators is to reflect these changes introduced by Member States' experts in the remaining language versions of the document.

The flow of documents described above [2] has several implications for GSC translators' work. One implication is that very little is translated from scratch. There is a large amount of repetition and interconnection among texts, both explicit and implicit intertextuality (see also Koskinen 2000: 59, Robertson 2015: 42). That is why consistency of terminology and phraseology both inside one document as well as across documents is paramount.

Another implication is that the documents translated are often working or interim versions drawn up in a hurry by non-native English speakers, not final, well-edited and fine-tuned texts.[3] This has one big advantage and one big drawback. The drawback is that the quality of source documents may not be ideal; the advantage is that should an error in translation be spotted after the translated document has been delivered to the client, translators may get a chance to correct it in the following version, if there is one.

Last but not least, this system of work has also implications for the setting of deadlines. As the translated documents are needed for a specific meeting or serve as input for further precisely scheduled work, translation deadlines need to be adapted to the requirements of document users, and can sometimes be very short. Often, they are set for a specific hour of the very same day.[4]

[2]This is the standard flow of legal and political documents. Apart from these, the GSC's Translation Service also translates other documents like agendas, minutes, speeches, web articles, etc., which are naturally produced in a different way. Nevertheless, even these documents often rely on their previous versions or related legal or political texts, so even in their case the level of intertextuality as indicated by the *document compare* remains quite high.

[3]See Stefaniak (2013) for a similar remark concerning texts translated by the European Commission.

[4]In 2016, translations with a deadline shorter than one day accounted for around 45% of all translated documents; in terms of net pages, their share was around 20% (Council of the European Union, General Secretariat 2017).

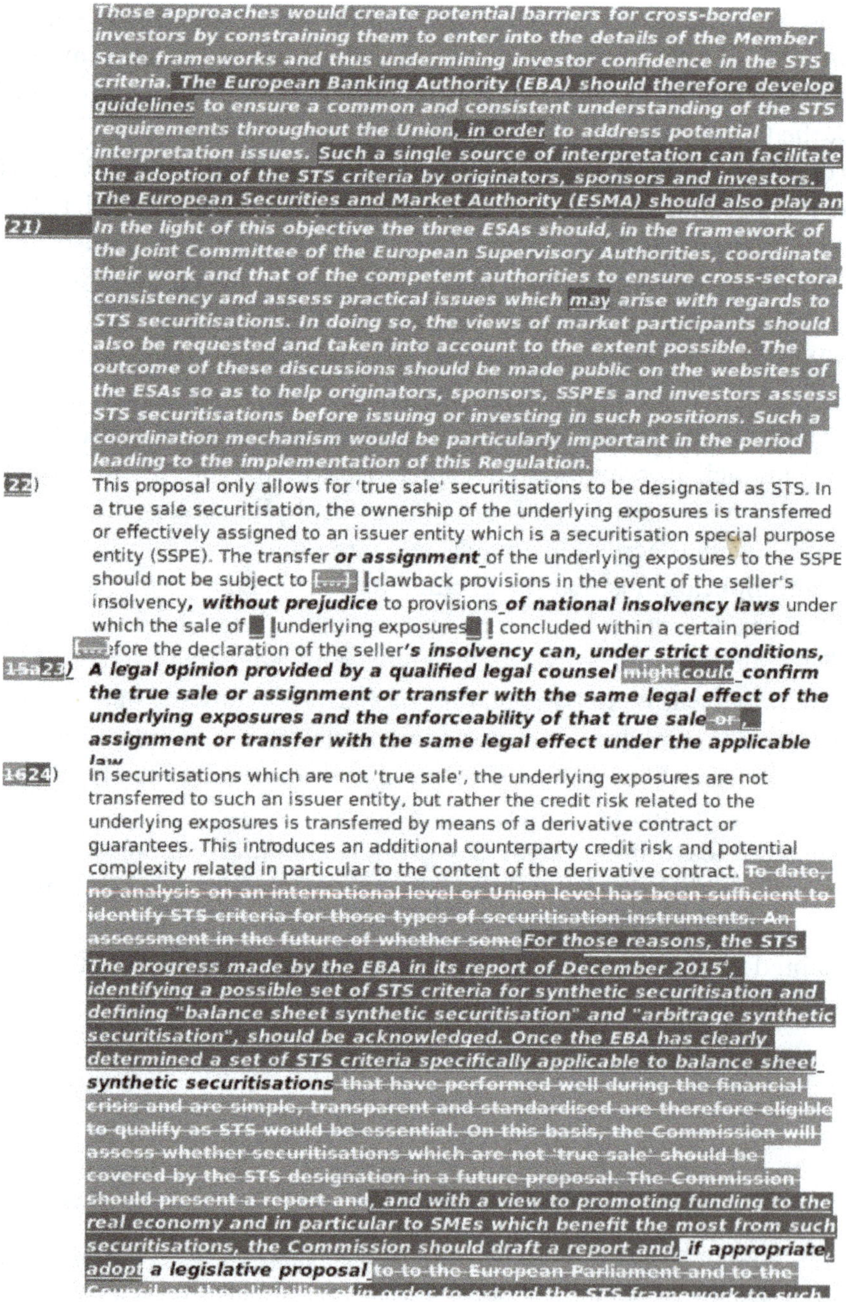

Those approaches would create potential barriers for cross-border investors by constraining them to enter into the details of the Member State frameworks and thus undermining investor confidence in the STS criteria. The European Banking Authority (EBA) should therefore develop guidelines to ensure a common and consistent understanding of the STS requirements throughout the Union, in order to address potential interpretation issues. Such a single source of interpretation can facilitate the adoption of the STS criteria by originators, sponsors and investors. The European Securities and Market Authority (ESMA) should also play an

21) *In the light of this objective the three ESAs should, in the framework of the Joint Committee of the European Supervisory Authorities, coordinate their work and that of the competent authorities to ensure cross-sectoral consistency and assess practical issues which may arise with regards to STS securitisations. In doing so, the views of market participants should also be requested and taken into account to the extent possible. The outcome of these discussions should be made public on the websites of the ESAs so as to help originators, sponsors, SSPEs and investors assess STS securitisations before issuing or investing in such positions. Such a coordination mechanism would be particularly important in the period leading to the implementation of this Regulation.*

22) This proposal only allows for 'true sale' securitisations to be designated as STS. In a true sale securitisation, the ownership of the underlying exposures is transferred or effectively assigned to an issuer entity which is a securitisation special purpose entity (SSPE). The transfer ***or assignment*** of the underlying exposures to the SSPE should not be subject to [....] clawback provisions in the event of the seller's insolvency***, without prejudice*** to provisions ***of national insolvency laws*** under which the sale of underlying exposures concluded within a certain period [....]efore the declaration of the seller***'s insolvency can, under strict conditions,***

15a23) ***A legal opinion provided by a qualified legal counsel ~~might~~could confirm the true sale or assignment or transfer with the same legal effect of the underlying exposures and the enforceability of that true sale ~~or~~, assignment or transfer with the same legal effect under the applicable law***

1624) In securitisations which are not 'true sale', the underlying exposures are not transferred to such an issuer entity, but rather the credit risk related to the underlying exposures is transferred by means of a derivative contract or guarantees. This introduces an additional counterparty credit risk and potential complexity related in particular to the content of the derivative contract. ~~To date, no analysis on an international level or Union level has been sufficient to identify STS criteria for those types of securitisation instruments. An assessment in the future of whether some~~*For those reasons, the STS The progress made by the EBA in its report of December 2015[4], identifying a possible set of STS criteria for synthetic securitisation and defining "balance sheet synthetic securitisation" and "arbitrage synthetic securitisation", should be acknowledged. Once the EBA has clearly determined a set of STS criteria specifically applicable to balance sheet* ***synthetic securitisations*** ~~that have performed well during the financial crisis and are simple, transparent and standardised are therefore eligible to qualify as STS would be essential. On this basis, the Commission will assess whether securitisations which are not 'true sale' should be covered by the STS designation in a future proposal. The Commission should present a report and~~*, and with a view to promoting funding to the real economy and in particular to SMEs which benefit the most from such securitisations, the Commission should draft a report and,* ***if appropriate,*** *adopt* ***a legislative proposal*** ~~to to the European Parliament and to the Council on the eligibility of~~ *in order to extend the STS framework to such*

Figure 1: The "Document compare" working mode.

2 The pragmatic approach to translation quality

The GSC's Translation Service aims to deliver end products which transpose – into the target language and by the set deadline – the entire contents of the source document with clarity, fluency and precision, in terms of form and content, without any formal or material errors, and without any additions or omissions, while taking into account the nature and the relative importance of the original to be translated (Council of the European Union, General Secretariat 2006: 4). This definition of translation quality is similar to the ISO Standard 17100 on Requirements for translation services (2015). However, the aim of the GSC's Translation Service is not to apply for ISO certification, but rather to ensure that its practice is broadly in line with international standards in the profession.

In essence, the GSC Translation Service's qualitative requirements, stemming from the above definition, can be roughly divided into three categories (see also the quality monitoring criteria in part 5 of this chapter). First, there are, naturally, **linguistic** aspects ("... [transpose] the entire contents of the source document with clarity, fluency and precision ..."). However, one of the findings from quality monitoring is that translators sometimes become fixated on the linguistic quality at the expense of everything else. This is why GSC's translators are kept aware that apart from linguistic aspects their translation work has at least two other qualitative dimensions.

Technical quality aspects ('... *in terms of form* ...') include requirements that the layout of a translation correspond to that of the original and that technical and typographical conventions of the target language be respected. At the Council and its preparatory bodies specifically, parallel pagination of the different language versions of a text for instance is not just a formal requirement but a practical necessity. As there are usually at least 28 delegations discussing and expressing themselves on a particular document, it is absolutely crucial for all of them to be on the same page at least in the text, if not mentally. Otherwise their communication might collapse. Compliance with the technical requirement to use computer-aided translation tools also makes translations easier to recycle and helps to preserve the necessary continuity and terminological consistency within and among documents.

Finally, **timeliness** ('... *by the set deadline* ...') is the third inherent part of quality requirements for the GSC translation. It follows from a legal provision stipulating that ministers or ambassadors can generally vote only on documents which are available in all official languages. A missing language version can therefore complicate or paralyze the whole decision-making process at the Council, and in such a case even a top-notch linguistic quality of a translation cannot compensate for its late submission.

Owing to the omnipresent pressure on public institutions to use resources efficiently, translation quality measures need to be directed towards achieving an optimal level of useful quality, fit for the intended purpose of the document. Hence the above definition of translation quality is implemented through the concept of fitness for purpose: a translation is considered fit for purpose when it is suitable for its intended communicative use, follows the linguistic and technical specifications and complies with the expressed and implied requirements of the client[5] (Council of the European Union, General Secretariat 2015: 36).

What this principle of fitness for purpose means in practice is that the efforts devoted to spotting and correcting errors must be adjusted to the type of text in question. If there is a wrong date in a translation (e.g. 13 May instead of 31 May) in a footnote reference to published legislation (where everything else is correct), it is objectively a translation error, but not a serious one as the reader will still be able to find the relevant document with all the other information. A similar error in the summary minutes of a meeting which is intended for its participants could create some confusion, but once again it would not be considered very important as the participants know when the meeting took place. However, a wrong date in a translation of a notice of meeting would be very serious as it can result in delegates turning up on the wrong day. In this case, the same translation error, previously considered minor, would make the whole document unfit for its purpose.

3 Quality-enhancing tools and procedures

A number of tools and procedures are in place at the GSC's Translation Service to help translators achieve the required quality of their translations.

First, there are tools helping to ensure the necessary consistency of terminology, phraseology and style as well as to make the translation process more efficient. These include translation memory and other computer-aided translation tools, databases of translated documents (e.g. Eur-Lex), terminological databases (e.g. IATE) and other databases (e.g. lists of government members) as well as vari-

[5] The main clients of the GSC's Translation Service are the European Council and its President, the rotating presidencies of the Council of the EU, the Council and its preparatory bodies, the requesting departments in the Directorates-General of the GSC, Member States' delegations and national administrations, other EU institutions, the European External Action Service, stakeholders in the subject areas concerned, and the general public.

ous style guides (*Inter-institutional Style Guide* (Publications Office 2011), *Manual of Precedents for Acts Established within the Council of the European Union* (Council of the European Union, General Secretariat 2010b), web translation guidelines (e.g. Council of the European Union, General Secretariat 2016a). These tools do not need to be discussed in detail here, as translation memories, databases and style guides are standard equipment of any major in-house translation department and are also discussed in the preceding chapters in this book (e.g. Svoboda on style guides).

Second, as it is common in translation practice, most translations are revised by a second pair of eyes. The GSC's Translation Service uses five levels of revision: (1) **thorough revision**, which is used only for the most important documents, such as the European Council conclusions and major political declarations or statements of its President, accession treaties, etc., and includes both bilingual revision and monolingual review; (2) **"standard" revision**, i.e. bilingual examination of the target language content against the source language content; (3) **light revision**, which combines monolingual review of the whole document and a bilingual revision of potentially problematic or most important parts; (4) **review**, i.e. monolingual examination of the target text; and (5) **optional revision**, where for reasons of efficiency no revision or review is carried out unless the translator asks for it.[6]

Third, GSC's translators may consult drafters if they are not sure about the correct meaning of a particular sentence in the original text. The translators' questions are gathered centrally in order to avoid repetition, sent to relevant administrators whose replies are then shared between all the translators working on the relevant document by means of a Microsoft SharePoint platform on the corporate intranet. This practice helps to improve the quality of Council documents in general, because it makes it possible to spot and correct mistakes that may appear also in the originals. Furthermore, GSC's translators may usually ask national experts for terminological advice and benefit from their expert knowledge already when working on a translation.

Specialization is another way that helps to ensure the necessary quality of GSC's translations. Therefore, GSC's translators have formed the so-called **functional groups**. Basically, there are four of them and they mirror the most important Council configurations – economy and finance, environment (which also includes agriculture and energy), foreign and security policy, justice and home

[6]At the GSC's Translation Service, the terms *revision* and *review* are used as defined in the ISO Standard 17100 (2015). For a comparison of revision with the European Commission see Martin (2007).

affairs. Based on their education or areas of interest, translators are encouraged to join one of these groups, and subsequently to try to keep track of developments in their particular area. They also attend lectures to improve their knowledge in their field of specialization in general, as well as briefings on the most important specific legislative files that are going to be translated.

Similarly, the way documents are allocated for translation and revision can also contribute to the quality of their translation. As explained above, one given file can move backwards and forwards between the preparatory bodies of the Council and the Translation Service several times. Whenever possible, that particular file will be assigned to the same translators and revisers who know it from the previous rounds and can therefore deal with it better and faster. Obviously, this practice has its limits because at certain moments some translators would be overloaded while others left with nothing to do, but in terms of quality (and also job satisfaction) it has definitely proved its merits.

Finally, one more resource used at the GSC's Translation Service deserves special attention. The Quality Controllers of the GSC's Translation Service have drawn up and maintain a catalogue of Council documents which contains a taxonomy of documents translated in the GSC's Translation Service as well as best practices recommended for the translation of each type of document (Council of the European Union, General Secretariat 2010a). The translation recommendations follow from the assessment of political visibility and potential for legal and/or financial impact of each type of document, i.e. two variables which largely define the "fit for purpose" criterion.

Altogether, the catalogue identifies over 25 types of documents,[7] and, in addition to the best practices recommended generally, individual language units are allowed to add their own language-specific recommendations, if they consider it useful.

4 Ex-post quality monitoring

In 2006, a special report (9/2006) by the European Court of Auditors recommended that the GSC put in place both quantity and quality performance in-

[7]The exact number evolves over time. Apart from the two types mentioned in Figures 2 and 3, respectively, other document types include, for example, draft legislation at certain milestone stages, documents for adoption or discussion by the Council, Council minutes, declarations/statements by the High Representative or by the President of the European Council, appointments, manuals for use by national departments in Member States, speaking notes for the presidency, press releases, informative documents intended for the general public, such as brochures or various web content, etc.

EUROPEAN COUNCIL CONCLUSIONS

- **Political visibility**
  - Very high
- **Potential for legal / financial impact**
  - Low
- **Recommended level of revision**
  - Thorough
- **Minimum level of revision**
  - Thorough
- **Recommended best practices**
  - (...) The members of the summit teams should, whenever possible, translate the guidelines for conclusions and preliminary drafts of the conclusions in the run-up to the summit; in any case all members of the summit team should read the draft conclusions before the summit and, where necessary, discuss the main translation issues (...).

Figure 2: Example of best practices for the European Council conclusions

dicators for its translation work (Court of Auditors 2006). Consequently, results quality monitoring was introduced in 2009. It is a regular and systematic monitoring of representative samples of translations that leave the GSC's Translation Service. Every week a random sample of 20 pages from at least 5 different documents is selected and the fitness for purpose of their translations into all languages is evaluated by Quality Controllers or delegated senior translators. All pages are equally likely to be chosen. The evaluated samples are discussed at weekly meetings of Quality Controllers, and this is a way of ensuring a certain degree of harmonization of criteria across different evaluators working in different languages. Dealing with problems detected varies from one case to another. It can involve sending a terminology note to a whole language unit, issuing joint

AGENDAS FOR THE COUNCIL / COREPER / CSA / PSC

- **Political visibility**
  - Low
- **Potential for legal / financial impact**
  - Low
- **Recommended level of revision**
  - Optional
- **Minimum level of revision**
  - Optional
- **Recommended best practices**
  - Date and place of the meeting should be double checked. Where the reference document exists, the agenda item title should correspond to the title of the reference document, with no modifications or improvements. However, typos and serious grammar mistakes should be corrected.

Figure 3: Example of best practices for agendas

requests for corrigenda, reviewing of best practices in place, and so on (Council of the European Union, General Secretariat 2015: 72).

While the goal of the GSC's Translation Service is to have the proportion of pages considered "fit for purpose" as close as possible to 100%, it is important to emphasize that the overall objective of results quality monitoring is to serve as a diagnostic tool providing warning of potential problems which can still be corrected, rather than to cause a fixation on a specific figure.

In addition to results quality monitoring, individual quality monitoring was introduced in 2013 to help assess the quality of work of individual translators. For each translator, at least 20 pages of translation and 15 pages of revision, coming from at least 5 different documents, are evaluated by their Quality Controller each year. Both results quality monitoring and individual quality monitoring are based on the same sets of criteria: linguistic (meaning, omission, terminology, grammar, style) and technical (styles, characters, typos, other). Reports from individual quality monitoring should document both strengths and weaknesses of the translation assessed across these categories, and the results of the evaluation are always discussed with the translator concerned (Council of the European Union, General Secretariat 2015: 72). The main purpose of individual quality monitoring is to provide translators with systematic feedback.

5 The special case of European Council conclusions

The conclusions of the European Council are the most visible and politically sensitive document type that the GSC's Translation Service produces. These conclusions are always immediately scrutinized by politicians, journalists and analysts and their implications are widely discussed in the media. Moreover, it is also a document which is translated completely under the responsibility of the GSC Translation Service – unlike, for example, legislative acts, where many other actors (translators from other institutions, lawyer-linguists, national experts) are involved and where the GSC translators are responsible only for a part of the bulk of translation work. For these reasons, the GSC's Translation Service has always handled the European Council conclusions with special care.

Such special care has been even enhanced since 2012, after one unfortunate incident. An omission of one word in the French translation of the Euro Area Summit Statement of 29 June 2012 reportedly caused a certain degree of confusion in communication between the German Chancellor and the French President (Rousselin 2012). The disputed sentence in the English original reads as follows:

> When an effective single supervisory mechanism is established, involving the ECB, for banks in the euro area the ESM could, following a regular decision, have the possibility to recapitalize banks directly.

The same sentence in the French version of the statement originally read as follows:

> Lorsqu'un mécanisme de surveillance unique, auquel sera associée la BCE, aura été créé pour les banques de la zone euro, le MES pourrait, à la suite d'une décision ordinaire, avoir la possibilité de recapitaliser directement les banques.
>
> [Backtranslation into English: When a single supervisory mechanism is established, involving the ECB, for banks in the euro area the ESM could, following a regular decision, have the possibility to recapitalize banks directly.]

The bone of contention was the issue of when the Eurozone's EUR 500bn rescue fund, the European Stability Mechanism, would be able to pump cash directly into failing banks. The French version, where the information borne by the English word "effective" was missing, implied that the date in question would be 1 January 2013, when the structure of the single supervisory mechanism was due to be formally set up. However, the single supervisory mechanism became "effective", i.e. actually started performing its tasks, only on 4 November 2014 (European Central Bank 2014); in the meantime, it was necessary, among other things, to carry out a comprehensive assessment of all the banks subjected to the single supervision so that the new supervisory mechanism could start with a clean slate and no skeletons in the banks' cupboards. The amount at stake was reportedly worth EUR 40bn.

As a result of this, a new procedure for "pre-reading" summit conclusions was established at the GSC's Translation Service at the end of 2012. It works like this:

The first draft of conclusions is translated at the GSC's Translation Service and sent to national capitals in the week before the summit. Before its translation, the terminology department of the GSC's Translation Service extracts important terms from the draft and provides useful terminological hints or recommendations, usually via updated entries in IATE. Moreover, the terminologists establish a list of documents to which the conclusions refer, so that translators can find them more quickly and easily. During their translation work, translators of the first draft send questions to quality coordinators whenever they encounter any ambiguity in the text or whenever they are not sure about the intended meaning of a particular sentence. After that, quality coordinators and terminologists meet to discuss the translation issues that emerged. Either they are able to solve them among themselves, or they send questions to the drafter, who, in turn, either provides the correct answer or helps to clarify the intended meaning, or in some cases redrafts the problematic parts in the following version of the conclusions.

Furthermore, one day ahead of the summit, before the last pre-summit draft is sent for translation, the translators who are going to work on the summit team meet with the relevant administrator who informs them of the expected course of the summit, explains which parts of the conclusions are the most contentious and why, and also answers additional questions that may have arisen in the meantime.

The final text agreed during the summit is, however, completely in the hands of the two or three translators (per language unit) working on the summit team. Here the deadline is extremely short, so there is no more time for consultations. Fortunately, the very last version is usually not much different from the penultimate version. At this final stage, focus is paramount, because here the task is to incorporate all the changes, no matter how small, in the correct place in the text as quickly as possible.

Generally, the pre-reading of the European Council conclusions has been helping to improve both the quality of the original text – where errors and unintended ambiguities can be spotted and corrected at an early stage – and the quality of its translations – where uniform interpretation and the use of correct terminology are enhanced.

6 Conclusion

The aim of this chapter has been to illustrate how the GSC's Translation Service manages the quality of the translations it produces. Its approach is a pragmatic one, which takes into account the importance of individual documents and the needs of their users. Being aware that anybody can make a mistake, the GSC's Translation Service has set up tools and procedures to minimize their occurrence, or practical impact if they happen.

The quality-enhancing tools and procedures at the GSC's Translation Service include the use of style guides, computer-aided translation tools and various databases to ensure the necessary consistency of terminology, phraseology and style both within and across documents. Translations are generally revised by a second pair of eyes, and for this purpose five levels of revision thoroughness have been defined and are applied depending on the type and importance of a particular document. The quality of translations is further enhanced by a possibility for translators to communicate with drafters of the originals, by specialization of translators as well as by allocation of documents for translators and/or revisers based on their involvement in the work on previous versions of the same file. Last but not least, a taxonomy of documents translated in the GSC's Translation Service has been compiled and provides, for each type of document, best practices recommended for its translation and revision. Special care, including a collective pre-reading of the original text, centralized terminological research and a meeting with the drafter, is dedicated to the GSC Translation Service's hallmark product – the European Council conclusions.

The quality of translations produced at the GSC's Translation Service is systematically monitored and evaluated. To this end, a tool to provide qualitative performance indicators has been introduced. We are not aware of any other large translation organization which would be monitoring the quality of its output by means of systematic random sampling.

References

Council of the European Union, General Secretariat. 2006. *Framework note on quality policy(internal document).*

Council of the European Union, General Secretariat. 2010a. *Document-specific Best Practices (internal document).*

Council of the European Union, General Secretariat. 2010b. *Manual of precedents for acts established within the Council of the European Union (internal document).*

Council of the European Union, General Secretariat. 2015. *Guide to the translation service (internal document).*

Council of the European Union, General Secretariat. 2016a. *DG F1 web style guide (internal document).*

Council of the European Union, General Secretariat. 2016b. *DGA 3 annual report 2015 (internal document).*

Council of the European Union, General Secretariat. 2017. *DGA 3 statistics 2016 (internal document).*

European Central Bank. 2014. *ECB assumes responsibility for euro area banking supervision. ECB Press Release, 4 November 2014.* https://www.ecb.europa.eu/press/pr/date/2014/html/pr141104.en.html, accessed 2017-8-24.

European Court of Auditors. 2006. Special Report No 9/2006 concerning translation expenditure incurred by the Commission, the Parliament and the Council. *Official Journal of the European Union* (C 284).

ISO 17100:2015. 2015. *Translation services – Requirements for translation services.* Geneva: ISO. http://www.iso.org/iso/catalogue_detail.htm?csnumber=59149.

Koskinen, Kaisa. 2000. Institutional illusions. translating in the EU Commission. *The Translator* 6(1). 49–65.

Martin, Tim. 2007. Managing risks and resources: a down-to-earth view of revision. *The Journal of Specialised Translation* 8. 57–63.

Publications Office of the European Union. 2011. *Interinstitutional style guide.* http://publications.europa.eu/code/en/en-000500.htm, accessed 2017-9-19.

Robertson, Colin. 2015. Eu multilingual law: interfaces of law, language and culture. In Susan Šarčević (ed.), *Language and culture in EU law. Multidisciplinary perspectives,* 33–51. Farnham: Ashgate.

Rousselin, Pierre. 2012. Sommet européen: le mot qui fâche Merkel et Hollande. *Le Figaro* 18 October 2012. http://www.lefigaro.fr/conjoncture/2012/10/18/20002-20121018ARTFIG00667-sommet-europeen-le-motqui-fache-merkel-et-hollande.php, accessed 2017-8-24.

Stefaniak, Karolina. 2013. Multilingual legal drafting, translators' choices and the principle of lesser evil. *Meta. The Translators' Journal* 58(1). 58–65.

Svoboda, Tomáš. 2013. Translation manuals and drafting style guides at the European Commission. *Le Bulletin du CRATIL Centre de recherche de l'ISIT* 10. http://www.lebulletinducratil.fr/index.php/en/translation-manuals-and-drafting-style-guides-at-the-european-commission, accessed 2017-8-30.

Chapter 9

Two-tiered approach to quality assurance in legal translation at the Court of Justice of the European Union

Dariusz Koźbiał
University of Warsaw

The objective of this chapter is to identify the key aspects of Quality Assurance (QA) affecting the quality of translations at the Court of Justice of the European Union (CJEU). The chapter starts with a brief clarification of the terms connected with QA, which are quite often used interchangeably and imprecisely. The next two sections set the background for the analysis by exploring the current language arrangements at the CJEU and associated challenges, and by discussing two standards that are relevant to the field of legal translation, namely EN 15038:2006 and ISO 17100:2015. The main part of the chapter proposes a two-tiered approach to translation quality at the CJEU. It is argued that it can be conceptualized at two interrelated levels, namely the human resources level and workflow level. While the human resources level comprises, inter alia, in-house lawyer-linguists, external contractors, revisers, auxiliary staff and project managers, the workflow level consists of measures aimed at achieving proper structurization of the translation process as well as intra- and interinstitutional co-operation.

1 Introduction

This chapter is aimed at identifying and evaluating the key quality aspects underlying the Quality Assurance strategy applied in the process of the translation of legal documents at the Court of Justice of the European Union (CJEU). However, owing to the fact that the terminology used in reference to Quality Management (QM) is still unclear (Lušicky & Wetzel 2017: 168), a crucial distinction has to be drawn between a number of mutually related terms, such as Quality Assurance

Dariusz Koźbiał. 2017. Two-tiered approach to quality assurance in legal translation at the Court of Justice of the European Union. In Tomáš Svoboda, Łucja Biel & Krzysztof Łoboda (eds.), *Quality aspects in institutional translation*, 155–174. Berlin: Language Science Press. DOI:10.5281/zenodo.1048198

(QA), Translation Quality Assessment (TQA) and Quality Control (QC), which are most widely used in discussions on quality in translation, as they are the key elements in QM systems (Lušicky & Wetzel 2017: 168).

The chapter does not consider aspects of TQA (also referred to as quality evaluation), which concerns itself with measuring and assessing the quality of an end product of the translation process (Drugan 2013: 76). In contrast, QA takes a broader look at the holistic process of translation and associated resources. As explained by Mossop (2014: 129):

> Quality assurance is the full set of procedures applied not just after (as with quality assessment) but also before and during the translation production process, by all members of a translating organization, to ensure that quality objectives important to clients are met.

Bearing the above explanation in mind, TQA could be regarded as strictly complementary to the general QA strategy adopted by a given institution or organization. Thus, QA refers to an all-encompassing system which aims at preventing quality-connected problems from occurring in the first place and is considered a *global* approach to translation quality at any stage of the translation process (Drugan 2013: 76). Another definition of QA is provided by Popiołek (2015: 342):

> QA (Quality Assurance) is a model approach that ensures good results if the right combination of human and technical resources is used in a sequence of steps and tasks that constitute a process within a system.

Popiołek's definition of QA emphasizes the central role of human resources as well as technical resources in the translation process viewed as a whole, thus emphasizing the viewpoint that any consistent approach to QA cannot be piecemeal.

On the other hand, the goal of QC is to verify whether the translation product or service meet stated quality specifications (Lušicky & Wetzel 2017: 169, in Lommel 2015 (ed.)). Therefore, TQA and QC enable verification of compliance with the planning and preventive measures set out in the general QA strategy (Lušicky & Wetzel 2017: 169).

For the purposes of this chapter, the QA strategy applied by the translation service (TS) of the CJEU is considered to rest on two key pillars, which enable the Court to communicate both internally and externally, namely human resources and workflow processes. Such a division will enable a thorough and critical evaluation of the Court's approach to QA with regard to the process of translation of its documents as well as the relation of the ISO 17100:2015 standard, which is currently the most relevant standard for QA in legal translation, to the said approach.

2 Language arrangements within the institution

Although the Court of Justice of the European Union (CJEU) is an EU institution which could be likened to a supreme or constitutional court of a Member State (Lord Roper & Lord Bowness 2011: 10; Itzcovich 2014), there are several crucial differences between the CJEU and Member States' supreme and constitutional courts. These differences consist not only in the respective courts' competences, as the CJEU's role is to settle issues connected primarily to EU law,[1] but also in the adapted language systems, which are predominantly monolingual in the case of Member States and multilingual in the case of the EU court. Despite this fact, the CJEU has to operate in a way that allows for full adoption of the multilingualism principle within its institutional setting and guarantees access to its case law, which constitutes a source of law in the Member States via a binding precedent (Łachacz & Mańko 2013: 86, Arnull 2006: 626–628, Sulikowski 2005: 221–232).

The current language arrangements at the Court make it a truly multilingual institution which has no counterpart in any other court, mainly due to the fact that, in direct actions, each of the 24 official languages of the European Union can be the language of a case brought before the Court, i.e. the language in which the proceedings will be conducted.[2] The CJEU's obligation to observe the principle of linguistic diversity arises from *inter alia* Regulation No 1 of the Council,[3] Article 3(3) of the Treaty on the EU,[4] dated 15 April 1958, under which the number of official languages has gradually increased as new Member States have joined the Community, and Article 22 of the Charter of Fundamental Rights of the EU,[5]

[1] As stated on the CJEU's website (https://curia.europa.eu/jcms/jcms/Jo2_6999/en/ accessed 2017-05-02), the Court's mission consists in ensuring that the Treaties are interpreted and applied according to EU law. The CJEU, inter alia, reviews the lawfulness of the acts of EU institutions, ensures that the Member States comply with obligations resulting from the Treaties, and interprets EU law at the request of the national courts and tribunals. Its competences include actions in areas such as competition, human rights, administrative, and constitutional law. The CJEU does not have criminal jurisdiction.

[2] Court of Justice – Presentation https://curia.europa.eu/jcms/jcms/Jo2_7024/en/ (accessed 2017-05-02.)

[3] Council Regulation No 1 of 15 April 1958 determining the languages to be used by the European Economic Community, Official Journal 017, 06/10/1958 P. 0385-0386

[4] Official Journal C 326, 26/10/2012 P. 0001–0390

[5] Charter of Fundamental Rights of the European Union OJ C 326, 26.10.2012, p. 391–407

which calls upon European institutions to respect linguistic diversity. It is also reflected in the CJEU's Statute (Article 64),[6] in the Rules of Procedure of the Court of Justice[7] and the General Court[8] (*language of the case*; Articles 36–42 and 44–49, respectively). The Rules of Procedure of the CJEU allow for the use of any one of all official EU languages as the language of the case. What needs to be emphasized is that the language of the case automatically becomes *the authentic language* of the documents, unless another language has been designated. The Rules of Procedure do not govern the use of languages within the administrative, internal activity of the Court. In order to guarantee equal access to justice for all citizens, it is essential for the parties to proceedings before the Court to be able to use their own language. Therefore, the CJEU has to communicate with the parties in the language of the proceedings and with the wider public using the EU's official languages, so that its case law is easily available to all EU citizens.

At the time of writing, the European Union (still) has 28 Member States and 24 official languages. Accordingly, upholding the principle of multilingualism requires that EU case law be published in all 24 official languages. However, as opposed to legislation, not all language versions of judgments are equally authoritative (cf. Kjær 2007: 69). Despite this fact, it is undisputed that legal translation plays a significant role in the functioning of EU institutions, especially within the CJEU's setting. Due to the fact that for historical reasons the CJEU's internal working language has been French (McAuliffe 2013a: 487, 2013b: 865), all procedural documents, pleadings and judgments need to be translated into this language. Since the creation of the CJEU in 1952, the linguistic situation at the Court has become more complex with each successive accession and the addition of new official languages, thus further increasing the total number of potential language combinations up to 552 (Annual Report, 2017).[9] This, however, does not mean that all documents need to be translated into all of the 24 official languages of the EU (cf. McAuliffe 2012, Künnecke 2013: 250). A case before the

---

[6]Consolidated version of Protocol (No 3) on the Statute of the Court of Justice of the European Union https://curia.europa.eu/jcms/upload/docs/application/pdf/2016-08/tra-doc-en-div-c-0000-2016-201606984-05_00.pdf (accessed 2017-05-02).

[7]Rules of Procedure of the Court of Justice of 25 September 2012 (OJ L 265, 29.9.2012), as amended on 18 June 2013 (OJ L 173, 26.6.2013, p. 65) and on 19 July 2016 (OJ L 217, 12.8.2016, p. 69) https://curia.europa.eu/jcms/upload/docs/application/pdf/2012-10/rp_en.pdf (accessed 2017-05-02.)

[8]Rules of procedure of the General Court OJ L 105, 23.4.2015, p. 1–66 http://eur-lex.europa.eu/legal-content/EN/TXT/?uri=uriserv:OJ.L_.2015.105.01.0001.01.ENG&toc=OJ:L:2015:105:TOC (accessed 2017-05-02)

[9]For comparison, the maximum number of language combinations in 1952 amounted to 12 language combinations.

Court may be examined in a single language, i.e. in the language of the case (applicant's language), unless any Member State intervenes, thus creating the need for translations into that Member State's official or designated language.

The legal translation service of the Court has to deal with ever-growing volumes of work. According to the data provided in the annual report for the year 2016 issued by the CJEU (Court of Justice of the European Union 2017a), the institution's Translation Service produced approximately 1,160,000 pages in the year under review. It needs to be pointed out that if it had not been for the introduction of internal economy measures aimed at reducing the amount of work, the total number of translated pages in 2016 would have reached 1,600,000.[10] If one compares this number of translated pages with the output of other EU institutions (e.g. in 2015, the European Commission's Directorate-General for Translation had an output of almost 2 million pages;[11] however, it can be assumed that a lesser portion of this amount constitutes legal translation considering the types of documents translated at the CJEU – cf. McAuliffe 2012), one can easily notice that legal translation is of paramount importance to the proper functioning of the Court. Uniform interpretation and application are perceived as critical determinants of quality when it comes to the translation of legal acts (Šarčević 1997: 73); however, it can be assumed that they are equally essential when it comes to the translation of case law and all types of procedural documents. Since the CJEU essentially seeks to persuade its audience, i.e. national legal communities (judges, lawyers, academics, etc.), in favor of its understanding of EU law, it needs to rely on translation so that its message can actually get across (Łachacz & Mańko 2013: 85, in Paunio 2007: 296). As observed by McAuliffe (2014: 9), the goal of translation at the CJEU is to produce parallel texts that will allow uniform interpretation and application by national courts; or in other words, that they will have the same effect in all Member States. Of course, one could assume that quality does not always go hand in hand with quantity (especially with such a high output as provided above); however, in order to ensure the smooth functioning of the Court, its TS not only needs to produce numerous translations within tight deadlines, but also needs to ensure that these translations are of high quality, which is made even more difficult by the complexity of the EU linguistic and legal context (Kjær 2007: 69), thus necessitating the proper selection of staff working at the Court's TS.

[10] Court of Justice of the European Union – Annual Report 2016 https://curia.europa.eu/jcms/upload/docs/application/pdf/2017-04/ragp-2016_final_en_web.pdf (accessed 2017-05-02).

[11] 2015 Annual Activity Report Directorate-General for Translation. 2016. (https://ec.europa.eu/info/sites/info/files/activity-report-2015-dg-t_april2016_en.pdf, accessed 2017-05-02).

There are several main reasons for the complexity of translation work done at the CJEU. Kjær (2007: 70) observes that difficulties connected with EU legal translation stem from the interplay of the legal systems of individual Member States and the fact that EU law (and thus also case law) does not constitute an established system, which is in fact still in fluctuation. In order to effectively and correctly translate texts which are originally created in such a complex environment, it is crucial for the legal translator to possess in-depth knowledge of the participant legal systems, legal languages as well as be able to compare them (Kjær 2007: 71). Kjær seems to have proposed a quite adequate term for the type of legal translation produced in the EU context, namely *supranational translation* (Kjær 2007: 76). This term conveys the fact that translation in the European Union concerns both translation within and between legal systems, because the EU legal system is still "under construction". The proposed term refers not only to the translation of legislation, but also to the translation of, inter alia, judgments of the CJEU and requests for preliminary rulings directed to the Court by national courts (Kjær 2007: 77). On top of that, both legislation and case law of the CJEU carry legal effects, which could be extremely harmful as a result of translations of bad quality – construction of case law (and therefore its translations) may affect the application of that law by national courts (McAuliffe 2013a: 492). With this in mind, it is clear that only highly specialized translators can be responsible for the type of translation described above. As Biel points out (2011a: 25), translations of legal texts need to be both "accurate and beautiful". She stresses the fact that translators transferring information conveyed in legal documents have to bear in mind both the equivalence relation, i.e. the relation between the source text and target text, as well as the relation of textual fit, i.e. the relation between the translated language and the naturally occurring non-translated language of a similar genre. The former is of vital importance, as it involves accuracy of the information transfer and use of correct terminology, whereas the latter concerns the naturalness of translations (Biel 2011a). Another problematic issue for legal translators concerns the standardization of legal terminology, which is difficult to achieve in a multilingual environment, where legal terminology expressed in 24 official languages is rooted in 28 national legal systems (Biel 2011a: 75, 79). Terminological problems are usually posed by incongruent levels of equivalence between legal concepts in the source and target legal systems (Prieto Ramos 2011: 16). The difference between the meaning of EU and national terminology has been stated by the Court of Justice in the CILFIT case:[12]

[12] Case C-283/81 – Judgment of the Court of 6 October 1982. - Srl CILFIT and Lanificio di Gavardo SpA v Ministry of Health [1982] ECR 3415, paragraph 19, http://eur-lex.europa.eu/

> It must be borne in mind [...] that Community law uses terminology which is peculiar to it and that legal concepts do not necessarily have the same meaning in Community law and in the law of the various Member States.

One type of solution to this problem are terminological databases, which are already being used at the Court. Terminological databases constitute a QA tool, because they allow translators to use appropriate terminology in a consistent manner within and across texts (Lušicky & Wetzel 2017: 166). Legal terminology, as a special feature of legal discourses, is seen as a central component of legal translation theory and practice (Prieto Ramos 2015: 15).

Another problematic issue concerns the sheer number of official languages currently in use in the European Union and its institutions. The accession of ten new states in the 2004 enlargement did not only entail the introduction of new legal traditions, thus necessitating a need for proper adjustment of the way of functioning of the Court, it also meant significant linguistic challenges (McAuliffe 2008: 812). The accession of new states and the addition of new languages spurred the Court on to amend its Rules of Procedure and reduce the number of pages published (and therefore translated) in the European Court Reports (McAuliffe 2008). Another change which resulted from the 2004 enlargement pertained to how Advocates General drafted their opinions – before 2004 they used to draft them in their mother tongue, but after 2004 some of the Advocates General started to draft opinions in the Court's pivot languages, which, in turn, influenced the style of the opinions, causing them to be more synthetic in nature (McAuliffe 2008: 816; McAuliffe 2010: 254, 2012: 9). The Court itself deliberates using the French language. For this reason, all procedural documents must be translated into French.

3 EN 15038:2006 and ISO 17100:2015 standards

Since attention to translation quality accelerated in the 1990s (Prieto Ramos 2015: 15), it translated into the willingness to establish standards encompassing the whole industry, which have become essential for assuring quality by means of systematic QM (Lušicky & Wetzel 2017: 170). It is worth taking a look at what the European Committee for Standardization (CEN) has worked out with regard to standardizing the approach to the quality of translations. In 2006, the CEN issued the EN 15038 standard entitled "Translation Services – Service Requirements"

legal-content/EN/TXT/?uri=CELEX%3A61981CJ0283 (accessed 2017-05-02).

(Mossop 2014: 131). It was the first pan-European standard regulating the quality of translation services (Biel 2011a: 16). It is worth noting that EN 15038 used to define quality rather indirectly, in its statement about the task of the reviser: "the reviser shall examine the translation for its suitability for purpose". The wording was unclear, for example, as to whether revision was required to include a comparative re-reading. However, the document did specify the requirement to revise every translation by a second translator (Biel 2011b).

On May 1, 2015, the ISO (International Organization for Standardization) issued the ISO 17100:2015 standard under the title "Translation services – Requirements for translation services", which extended the scope of and superseded the EN-15038 standard. The structure of ISO 17100:2015 has changed compared to EN 15038 and focuses more heavily on conventional translation processes. However, it still does not point out the exact qualities of a high-quality translation, as was also the case with the previous standard (cf. Biel 2011a: 18). The obligatory revision performed by a second person also remains key in the current standard. Performing a review remains optional. The translation service provider has to ensure that a final verification of the translation project is performed before it is delivered to the client. Besides the actual standard, there are also attachments which explain certain aspects of the standard by means of examples or graphical cues to help visualize the processes. The ISO 17100:2015 standard lists requirements for the core processes, resources and other aspects necessary for the provision of a quality translation service that meets applicable specifications, and therefore (same as the previous standard) is also perceived as a compendium of what should be done in order to contribute to Quality Assurance in translation, assuming that if the QA measures are in place, the end product of translation will be of good quality (cf. Gouadec 2010: 271). The use of raw output from machine translation plus post-editing is outside the scope of ISO 17100:2015; it also does not apply to interpreting services. It does not define *quality* per se; however, it does explain the meaning of the main concepts related to translation and translation services, translation workflow and technology, language and content, human resources involved in the provision of translation services, and control of the process of delivering a translation service (ISO 17100:2015:2015). The ISO 17100:2015:2015 standard also lays out guidelines concerning human (translators, revisers, reviewers, proofreaders and project managers) and technical and technological resources, pre-production processes and activities, the production process and post-production processes. Currently, the ISO 17100:2015:2015 standard is the most relevant standard applicable to QA in legal translation,[13] therefore, it will be referred to when discussing the key aspects underlying QA in the CJEU's TS's work.

As noted by Drugan (2013: 1), the establishment of objective criteria with regard to quality has always been a subject of general disagreement in Translation Studies, but it was indeed successful and led TSPs to apply standards in their work. It has to be noted, however, that some accidents may happen even in the most "quality-assured" environments (Gouadec 2010: 271), as some methodological problems may continue to appear even in institutional contexts in which QA measures have already been implemented (Prieto Ramos 2015: 12). What is more, the introduction and proper application of QA measures may be quite costly (Prieto Ramos 2015: 272). Nevertheless, QA is presumed to contribute to the production of translations characterized by higher quality. This chapter aims at discussing various aspects of QA practices in the work of the CJEU's translation service. It does not by any means attempt to be exhaustive and present a holistic approach to QA in the Directorate-General for Translation.

4 Two-tiered approach to Quality Assurance

In this chapter, it is argued that the general Quality Assurance policy in the Court's Directorate-General for Translation is based on two key pillars. This section proposes to conceptualize the notion of translation quality at the CJEU through two key pillars, namely human resources and well-structured workflow processes. While the human resources level comprises, inter alia, in-house lawyer-linguists, external contractors, auxiliary staff and project managers, the workflow level consists of measures aimed at achieving proper structurization of the translation process as well as intra- and interinstitutional co-operation.

[13]It needs to be pointed out that there is currently another international standard being developed under the working name ISO 20771 "Legal and other specialist translation services". When completed and if adopted, it is supposed to provide the minimum requirements for the qualifications, competence, core processes, resources, training and other aspects necessary for the provision of *legal or other specialist translation services* of quality that meet applicable specifications (Popiołek 2016). It is expected to define the competences and qualifications of legal and other specialist translators, revisers and reviewers in the context of the process applied in legal and specialist translation and it will also address the specific professional and QA challenges in the area of legal translation (Popiołek 2016). Similarly to 17100:2015, ISO 20771 will deal with concepts related to translation and translation services, translation workflow and technology, language and content, the people (human resources) involved in translation services, and the concepts related to the control of the translation service process (Popiołek 2016).

4.1 Quality Assurance at the human resources level

Human resources constitute the first key pillar of QA in the Court's TS work, which includes translators, revisers, auxiliary staff, and project managers, etc.

Translators' work done in the institutional setting of a European organization is of paramount importance for the institution itself, since without translations done in a timely manner it would be able to communicate neither internally, nor externally. Therefore, translators are in a way representatives of institutions for which they work. As Koskinen (2008: 24) rightly pointed out with regard to her work done at the European Commission's Translation Service:

> The translated text is not mine, nor does it have my name on it: it belongs to the institution, and it bears the name of the institution on it. It is not my trustworthiness but the trustworthiness of the translating institution that will be maintained, enhanced or harmed by my translation. In the Commission, my words are not mine; **I am a spokesperson for the institution** [emphasis added].

The same applies to the work of translators working at the CJEU, for whom translation is not an individual, personal act, but a part of a collective process thanks to which the institution is able to communicate both with the outside world as well as within itself as a consequence of its obligation to observe the principle of multilingualism.

The work of the legal translation service of the CJEU is very complex and demanding due to the highly specialized nature of its tasks. The main reasons for this are the complicated language arrangements at the Court. Since this section focuses specifically on the CJEU's legal translation service, it examines the work of the Court's translators, that is lawyer-linguists, who are employed in this institution as opposed to lawyer-linguists employed in other institutions of the EU.[14] Lawyer-linguists' work differs from the work of translators working for most of the European institutions, who possess, in most of the cases, a degree in translation but not a law degree as in the case of lawyer-linguists; lawyer-linguists' work consists mainly of legal translation exclusively into their mother tongue (McAuliffe 2016: 15) and the legal-linguistic revision of court documents, such as: applications or references for a preliminary ruling, written observations, reports for hearings, Advocate Generals' opinions and judgments of the Court.

[14] Apart from the Court of Justice of the EU lawyer-linguists work for the European Commission, the Council of the European Union, the European Parliament and the European Central Bank.

Since the CJEU's decisions need to be properly understood by courts in the national context of Member States, it seems reasonable that the task of translation has been devolved to national lawyers who are in the best position to act as mediators in the Court's communication with national courts (Łachacz & Mańko 2013: 85–86). This is thanks to their belonging to the same community as the target audience and their ability to interpret and translate the Court's messages in a way that allows them to retain their intended persuasive value (Łachacz & Mańko 2013). For this reason alone, translations into all of the official languages need to be of the highest possible quality.

Owing to the nature of documents translated at the CJEU and the constant interplay between law and legal translation, it is crucial that lawyer-linguists have legal thematic competence, which constitutes a distinctive feature of legal translation competence (Prieto Ramos 2011: 11). Article 42 of the Rules of Procedure of the Court of Justice specifies who is to form its translation service:

> The Court shall set up a language service staffed by experts with adequate legal training and a thorough knowledge of several official languages of the European Union.

Those who want to work as either in-house lawyer-linguists or external contractors need to meet strict requirements – essentially they need to have a law degree from their home country and have perfect command of at least two official languages apart from their mother tongue (McAuliffe 2016: 10). Lawyer-linguists should also be adept in the exercise of comparative law and be able to draft legal texts in their own languages. Since most of the documents translated at the Court are part of judicial proceedings, they carry specific legal effects. Any subpar quality of translated documents might, for instance, mislead national courts and institutions or potentially cause delays in the proceedings (Izzo Clarke 2014a: 9). Therefore, translations of appropriate quality need to not only convey the message of the original text, but also contain the right terminology (which might be specific to either the EU legal system or national legal systems), be free of grammatical and language errors as well as be written in the appropriate legal style. Lawyer-linguists should also be able to critically analyze translated documents both from a legal and linguistic perspective; they should always be on the lookout for any inconsistencies in the original texts in order to point out flaws to the authors of translated documents. Apart from the knowledge of EU and national legal systems and languages, lawyer-linguists must also possess interpersonal skills, intercultural competence and high ethical standards.

The entity responsible for the recruitment of lawyer-linguists[15] (as well as computer specialists, secretarial assistants, etc.) is the European Personnel Selection Office (EPSO). Therefore, in the light of the ISO 17100:2015 standard, the CJEU's legal translation service as the translation service provider is not burdened with the task of selecting the people who are to perform translation tasks as lawyer-linguists. Most of the lawyer-linguists employed in all language units are Permanent Officials who belong to appropriate AD function groups based on their work experience.[16] After the successful conclusion of the EPSO procedure, selected candidates begin their probationary period in which they are trained in-house and work under the supervision of a senior lawyer-linguist. Tutorship allows new lawyer-linguists to learn the working methods of their respective language units and practical issues connected with the translation of court documents. After the probationary period ends with a positive result, the lawyer-linguist becomes a full-grown EU official, whose duty is to continue to further hone their skills with regard to translation, terminology and comparative law. As a means of ensuring quality with regard to lawyer-linguists' output, their work is subject to yearly evaluation.

In order to cope with the increasing workload, the Court uses temporary or contract staff to perform auxiliary tasks. Temporary or contract staff cannot be in active employment as officials or other servants of the European Union when carrying out the specific work assignments described in framework contracts (Court of Justice of the European Union 2017b: 16). Contract staff working on outsourced translations also need to meet strict quality requirements, since their translations of legal documents have to be of high quality allowing for immediate publication or any other application (Court of Justice of the European Union 2017b: 16). As stated in the framework contract for the provision of translation services available at the Court's website, contract staff are required to ensure (Court of Justice of the European Union 2017b: 11):

1. compliance with specific instructions given by the Court;
2. correct, rigorous and precise use of the target language;

[15] DGT employs around 985 persons, of whom 613 are lawyer-linguists working in 23 language divisions. Thus, DGT staff represent 45 per cent of the whole staff of the Court (ca. 2,168). There is no separate Irish language division, as this forms a part of the English language division. (Information valid as of December 31, 2016. Source: https://curia.europa.eu/jcms/jcms/P_80908/en/; https://curia.europa.eu/jcms/upload/docs/application/pdf/2017-04/ragp-2016_final_en_web.pdf, accessed 2017-05-02.)

[16] http://europa.eu/epso/doc/staff_cat_graph.pdf (accessed 2017-05-02.)

3. rigorous use of the appropriate legal language and terminology of the target language;
4. strict use of the legal terminology used in the reference documents (source and target languages);
5. rigorous citation of the relevant legislative and/or judicial texts;
6. use of the necessary legal databases (of the European Union and national);
7. compliance with the Vade-Mecum of the Court (if appropriate);
8. delivery within the period agreed and specified in the order form.

Contractors' work is subject to QC and failure to meet deadlines or the inadequate quality of completed assignments may lead to penalties described in the contract provisions (Court of Justice of the European Union 2017b: 11). If the contractor is unable to carry out the work assigned to them within the prescribed period, the contractor may be required to pay to the Court a penalty of 10 % of the total amount invoiced per calendar day of delay by means of a deduction from the payment to be made to the contractor (Articles 5.5.1–5.5.2 of the framework contract). As a result of inadequate quality of translations, i.e. translations not compliant with the requirements stated in Article 5.6 of the framework contract, established by quality controllers, the contractor's remuneration for the translation in question may be suspended and subject to further assessment. A definite confirmation of inadequacy in terms of the quality of a specific work assignment may lead to the Court's refusal to pay in full or in part for that assignment.

Moreover, contractors are obliged to protect the confidentiality of all information communicated to them in the course of the performance of contracts (Court of Justice of the European Union 2017b: 16). External contractors receive appropriate support and assistance from the respective language units (access to glossaries, terminological databases, ability to participate in occasional workshops organized in Member States, where the external collaborators live, etc.). Strict requirements imposed on external contractors seem to be in line with the guideline set out in the ISO 17100:2015 standard, which concerns full responsibility of the TSP, that is the CJEU's TS, for sub-contracted work.

4.2 Quality Assurance at the workflow level

Internal and external communication on the part of the Court is carried out by the Directorate-General for Translation, which provides high-quality translations of different kinds of court documents (pleadings, opinions, judgments, orders, etc.) within tight deadlines. In 2015 alone, the total output of all language units equaled to 1,113,427 translated pages, whereas there was a total of 1,114,838 incoming pages (+1.4% as compared to the previous year). Although it has been noted that the process of translation extends the time in which the Court needs to pass a decision and also creates a substantial burden of financial costs, access to the CJEU's case law by EU citizens and Member States' authorities remains essential (Lord Roper & Lord Bowness 2011: 23).

The CJEU's translation service consists of 23 language units organized into two directorates, namely Directorate A (CS, ET, ES, FR, HU, LT, MT, NL, PL, RO, SK) and Directorate B (BG, DA, DE, EL, EN, FI, HR, IT, LV, PT, SL, SV), which are shared between the Court of Justice and the General Court. As a result of the 2004 enlargement, which added nine new official languages, the Directorate General grew substantially in size. This required the introduction of a measure allowing the TS to guarantee coverage of all official languages – it turned out to be the pivot translation system (Šarčević & Robertson 2013: 184), the introduction of which was planned ahead of the 2004 enlargement.[17] The system itself consisted in using several "bigger" languages, that is English, French, German, Italian and Spanish, to produce translations which were then used to translate into the "smaller" languages of new Member States (McAuliffe 2008: 810–816).

All units are required to comply with rules and standards aimed at achieving harmonization. Each language unit at the Directorate-General for Translation achieves this thanks to its own management personnel, composed of the Head of a Unit, a Quality Controller, a Resources Manager and a Head of Local Coordination. Proper management is especially important due to the existence of a large number of official languages and tight deadlines for translating court documents. The post of a Quality Policy Coordinator working at the level of the Directorate-General for Translation allows for ensuring the harmonization of quality policies among individual language units.

The Quality Policy Coordinator organizes sessions during which Quality Controllers from all language units review random samples submitted by individual language units. It is common for all units to submit the same range of pages from a given document, which allows for the harmonization of criteria across all 24 languages. Such sessions enable Quality Controllers to discuss problematic areas among themselves, issue corrigenda, terminology notes to language units and to clarify quality guidelines.

The process of translating court documents involves three main stages, i.e. translation, revision and proofreading (Izzo Clarke 2014b). Before the actual

[17] The preparations began in 2011 when a new director took charge of the translation service.

translation work is begun, a special unit composed of assistants identifies already translated parts of the text or those parts which are similar to previous documents (frequently occurring phrases, quotes from legislation or case law, etc.). After this preliminary work is done, the findings are then made available to lawyer-linguists who start translating the texts.

The actual translation consists of three main stages: analysis of the original text, which allows the lawyer-linguist to get to know the subject of the document and identify potential translation difficulties, terminological research and identification of sources, actual translation of the text, and using the research and sources identified at the earlier stage (Izzo Clarke 2014b). It needs to be stressed that as a means of ensuring the high quality of translated documents, lawyer-linguists work exclusively into their own languages (Šarčević & Robertson 2013: 201, McAuliffe 2016: 15). After the translation has been completed, it is time for the revision process, which aims to ensure legal and conceptual coherence with the original text and with other related documents of the Court. Its purpose is to verify whether the translation procedure has been followed according to the internal guidelines. Finally, the last stage involves proofreading, which is undertaken by a "pair of fresh eyes". The goal of proofreading is to guarantee formal coherence of the translated text, which needs to correspond to the source text and linguistic correctness. The revision and proofreading stages make up the quality control part of the translation process.

There are other processes which indirectly form part of QC (Izzo Clarke 2014b). One such example are processes aimed at maintaining terminological uniformity. This is ensured by using terminology databases in all official languages.[18] The automatic translation of standard phrases is used, but this is not to be confused with rule-based or statistical machine translation software being used on a large scale to produce translations of legal texts.[19] Furthermore, seminars, meetings and conferences are regularly held, in which the lawyer-linguists or specialized guest speakers tackle particular legal topics for those involved in their translation.

Another key component of the QA process is perceived to be the co-operation between units and inter-institutional co-operation, which indirectly form a part

[18]See, e.g., InterActive Terminology for Europe (IATE) – The European Union's multilingual term base http://iate.europa.eu (accessed 2017-05-02). The Court of Justice of the European Union has its own internal comparative multilingual legal terminological database – CuriaTerm (Künnecke 2013: 259).

[19]Machine translation carried out with the help of MT@EC allows EU officials to receive quick, raw machine translations from and into any official EU language (further information can be found for example at https://ec.europa.eu/info/resources-partners/machine-translation-public-administrations-mtec_en (accessed 2017-05-02).

of the workflow process. In order to maintain the highest level of coherence with the translated documents of other EU institutions, the Court of Justice participates in a number of inter-institutional working groups, dealing with subjects such as training, human resources, translation techniques, and terminology. Inter-institutional co-operation allows smaller institutions to use the resources of the larger institutions, which allows for lawyer-linguists' expertise to be taken advantage of by the translation services of other EU institutions.

Such co-operation is, however, subject to certain restrictions (Court of Justice translation service 2010: 1). The first major constraint refers to the type of documents translated by lawyer-linguists at the Court, which are "complex and structurally different" (i.e. case law and procedural documents, Court of Justice translation service 2010) from what is translated by translators at the three legislative institutions (i.e. the European Parliament, the Council of the European Union and the European Commission), and the question of confidentiality. Since, for example, the EU institutions are often involved in the proceedings before the Court of Justice (CJ) or the General Court (GC), they are not allowed to translate their own pleadings (Court of Justice translation service 2010: 2). The second major restriction concerns the workload of the CJEU's translation service, which is shared between the CJ and the GC (Court of Justice translation service 2010: 2). High workload translates into the lower availability of the Court's TS for other institutions requesting assistance. Due to the high workload of the TS, it has been proposed that a part of translations generally outsourced to freelance translators with legal qualifications be entrusted to legally qualified translators in the TSs of some other EU institutions.

The goal of inter-institutional co-operation is to avoid translating the same procedural documents translated by the French language units of different EU institutions (Court of Justice translation service 2010: 3). Such a form of an arrangement allows to cut back on double translations.

The most important forms of inter-institutional co-operation which contribute to QA in general are: sharing the products of terminological work and inter-institutional training activities (Court of Justice translation service 2010: 3). The first measure contributes to the increased terminological consistency of documents translated by not only the CJEU, but also other institutions of the EU. The second measure, i.e. inter-institutional training activities, entails conducting seminars on substantive matters of the law as well as terminology by either CJEU lawyer-linguists or outside expert legal scholars or judges. Such training is also open to translators from the TSs of other EU institutions (Court of Justice translation service 2010: 3).

5 Conclusions

This chapter aimed at identifying the key aspects of Quality Assurance within the institutional setting of the CJEU. It has been argued that quality aspects can be grouped around two key pillars of QA, namely human resources and workflow processes. The human resources level comprises, inter alia, in-house lawyer-linguists, external contractors, auxiliary staff and project managers; the workflow level consists of measures aimed at achieving the proper structurization of the translation process as well as intra- and interinstitutional co-operation. Both pillars enable the Court's translation service to provide high-quality translations in a timely manner, as evidenced by the way of functioning of the Court, which must rely on translations in order to work properly due to the complicated language arrangements that are in place.

Considering the fact that ensuring quality in translation by means of assessing only the final translation product is not sufficient (Lušicky & Wetzel 2017: 279), the influence of the two discussed aspects of QA is perceived to have the most significant impact on the translation process and its effectiveness. I have described the current language arrangements at the Court of Justice of the European Union, which due to their complexity might be viewed as an additional difficulty in the process of the translation of court documents. Moreover, I have pointed out the importance of industry-wide standards in legal translation (cf. EN 15038:2006 and ISO 17100:2015:2015). Information on the profile of lawyer-linguists who are not "just" translators and external contractors translating outsourced documents, the rigorousness of criteria for the selection of prospective candidates and assessment of translation quality further show how complex and demanding the translation process is. Although faced with many challenges, the Court of Justice of the European Union and its legal translation service are able to perform all their tasks without any major problems. This is evidenced by the data presented in, for instance, annual reports, which points to the fact that the Court is able to communicate both internally as well as externally with the wider public in the European context.

Acknowledgment

This study was financed by research grant No. 2014/14/E/HS2/00782 from the National Science Centre, Poland.

References

Arnull, Anthony. 2006. *The European Union and its Court of Justice.* Oxford: Oxford University Press.

Biel, Łucja. 2011a. Jakość przekładu prawnego i prawniczego w świetle normy europejskiej PN-EN 15038 oraz hipotezy uniwersaliów translatorycznych [Quality of legal translation through the lens of EN 15038 standard and the hypotheses of translation universals]. *Rocznik Przekładoznawczy* 6. 13–28.

Biel, Łucja. 2011b. Training translators or translation service providers? EN 15038:2006 standard of translation services and its training implications. *The Journal of Specialised Translation* 16. 61–76.

Court of Justice of the European Union. 2017a. *Annual Report 2016. The year in Review.* https://curia.europa.eu/jcms/upload/docs/application/pdf/2017-04/ragp-2016_final_en_web.pdf, accessed 2017-5-2.

Court of Justice of the European Union. 2017b. *Framework contract for the provision of translation services.* https://curia.europa.eu/jcms/upload/docs/application/pdf/2017-01/0_7_2017_en_contrat_vf_10012017.pdf, accessed 2017-5-2.

Court of Justice translation service. 2010. *Annex – Specific features of the translation service of the Court of Justice and contributions to inter-institutional cooperation.* http://www.europarl.europa.eu/meetdocs/2009_2014/documents/budg/dv/2010_coj_0%202_annexe_/2010_coj_02_annexe_en.pdf, accessed 2017-5-2.

Drugan, Joanna. 2013. *Quality in professional translation: assessment and improvement.* London: Bloomsbury.

Gouadec, Daniel. 2010. Quality in translation. In Yves Gambier & van Doorslaer Luc (eds.), *Handbook of Translation Studies*, vol. 1, 270–275. Amsterdam: John Benjamins.

ISO 17100:2015. 2015. *Translation services – Requirements for translation services.* Geneva: ISO. http://www.iso.org/iso/catalogue_detail.htm?csnumber=59149.

Itzcovich, Giulio. 2014. *The European Court of Justice as a constitutional court. Legal reasoning in a comparative perspective.* Brescia: University of Brescia.

Izzo Clarke, Joseph. 2014a. *Ten years of judicial cooperation. Reflections of a decade of EU Membership: expectations, achievements, disappointments and the future.* Msida.

Izzo Clarke, Joseph. 2014b. *Translating justice. The ECJ perspective.* Paper presented at the QUALETRA Final Conference, KU Leuven, Antwerp, 16–17 October 2014.

Kjær, Anne Lise. 2007. Legal translation in the European Union: A research field in need of a new approach. In Krzysztof Kredens & Stanisław Goźdź-Roszkowski (eds.), *Language and the law: international outlooks*, 69–95. Frankfurt am Main: Peter Lang.

Koskinen, Kaisa. 2008. *Translating institutions. an ethnographic study of EU translation*. Manchester: St. Jerome.

Künnecke, Martina. 2013. Translation in the EU: Language and law in the EU's judicial labyrinth. *Maastricht Journal of European and Comparative Law* 20(2). 243–260.

Łachacz, Olga & Rafał Mańko. 2013. Multilingualism at the Court of Justice of the European Union: theoretical and practical aspects. *Studies in Logic, Grammar and Rhetoric* 34(1). 75–92.

Lommel, Arle (ed.). 2015. *Multidimensional quality metrics (mqm) definition*. DFKI. http://www.qt21.eu/mqm-definition/definition-2015-12-30.html, accessed 2017-5-2.

Lord Roper & Lord Bowness. 2011. *The Workload of the Court of Justice of the European Union*. London. https://www.publications.parliament.uk/pa/ld201011/ldselect/ldeucom/128/128.pdf, accessed 2017-5-2.

Lušicky, Vesna & Michael Wetzel. 2017. Quality assurance in multilingual legal terminological databases. *The Journal of Specialised Translation* 27. 164–188.

McAuliffe, Karen. 2008. Enlargement at the European Court of Justice: Law, language and translation. *European Law Journal* 14(6). 806–818.

McAuliffe, Karen. 2010. Language and the institutional dynamics of the Court of Justice of the European Communities: lawyer-linguists and the production of a multilingual jurisprudence. In Gueldry M. (ed.), *How globalizing professions deal with national languages: studies in cultural conflict and cooperation*, 239–263. Lewinston: The Edwin Mellen Press.

McAuliffe, Karen. 2012. Language and law in the European Union: The multilingual jurisprudence of the ECJ. In Lawrence Solan & Peter M. Tiersma (eds.), *The Oxford Handbook of Language and Law*. http://www.oxfordhandbooks.com/view/10.1093/oxfordhb/9780199572120.001.0001%20/oxfordhb-9780199572120-e-15, accessed 2017-5-2.

McAuliffe, Karen. 2013a. Precedent at the Court of Justice of the European Union: The linguistic aspect. *Law and Language: Current Legal Issues* 15. 483–493.

McAuliffe, Karen. 2013b. The limitations of a multilingual legal system. *International Journal for the Semiotics of Law* 26(4). 861–882.

McAuliffe, Karen. 2014. Translating ambiguity. *The Journal of Comparative Law* 9(2). https://ore.exeter.ac.uk/repository/bitstream/handle/10871/17022/translating%20ambiguity.pdf?sequence=2, accessed 2017-5-2.

McAuliffe, Karen. 2016. Hidden translators: The invisibility of translators and the influence of lawyer-linguists on the case law of the Court of Justice of the European Union. *Language and Law* 3(1). 5–29.

Mossop, Brian. 2014. *Revising and editing for translators.* 3rd edn. London: Routledge.

Paunio, Elina. 2007. The tower of Babel and the interpretation of EU law: Implications for equality of languages and legal certainty. In Thomas Wilhelmsson, Elina Paunio & Annika Pohjolainen (eds.), *Private law and the many cultures of Europe*, 385–402. Alphen aan den Rijn: Kluwer Law International.

Popiołek, Monika. 2015. Terminology management within a translation quality assurance process. In Hendrik J. Kockaert & Frieda Steurs (eds.), *Handbook of terminology*, vol. 1, 341–359. Amsterdam: John Benjamins.

Popiołek, Monika. 2016. *ISO Standards Framework for QA in Legal Translation.* Paper presented at the Translating Europe Workshop: Forum on Quality in Legal Translation, Warsaw, 6 June 2016.

Prieto Ramos, Fernando. 2011. Developing legal translation competence: An integrative process-oriented approach. *Comparative Legilinguistics* 5. 7–21.

Prieto Ramos, Fernando. 2015. Quality assurance in legal translation: evaluating process, competence and product in the pursuit of adequacy. *International Journal for the Semiotics of Law* 28. 11–30.

Šarčević, Susan. 1997. *New approach to legal translation.* The Hague: Kluwer Law International.

Šarčević, Susan & Colin Robertson. 2013. The work of lawyer-linguists in the EU Institutions. In Anabel Borja Albi & Fernando Prieto Ramos (eds.), *Legal translation in context: Professional issues and prospects*, 181–202.

for Standardization (CEN), European Committee. 2006. *EN 15038:2006 Translation services – service requirements.* Brussels: CEN.

Sulikowski, Adam. 2005. Tworzenie prawa przez Europejski Trybunał Sprawiedliwości. wybrane problemy [the creation of law by the European Court of Justice: selected aspects]. In Kaczor J. (ed.), *Teoria prawa europejskiego [theory of european law]*. 221–232. Wrocław: Wyd. Uniwersytetu Wrocławskiego.

Name index

Subject index

www.ingramcontent.com/pod-product-compliance
Lightning Source LLC
Chambersburg PA
CBHW080544110426
42813CB00006B/1199
* 9 7 8 3 9 6 1 1 0 0 2 1 7 *